Contents

One Pot Pasta 6

One-Pot Mediterranean Chicken 6

One-Pot Pizza Tortellini Bake 8

One-Pot Shrimp Scampi Orzo 9

One Pot Tuna Casserole 10

Spicy One-Pot Shakshouka 11

One-Pot Breakfast 12

Thai Style One-Pot 13

One-Pot Ham and Veggie Pasta 14

Vegan One-Pot Coconut Curry with Pasta and Vegetables 15

Quick One-Pot Chicken Alfredo 16

One-Pot Spaghetti with Meat Sauce 17

One-Pot Moroccan Shrimp Tagine 18

One-Pot White Chicken Chili 19

One-Pot Rice and Beef Pilaf 20

Easy One-Pot Chicken Alfredo 21

One-Pot Spinach Mushroom Lasagna 22

One-Pot Lebanese Chicken and Rice 23

One-Pot Cajun Chicken and Sausage Alfredo Pasta 24

One-Pot Chicken Enchilada Mac and Cheese 25

One Pot Thai-Style Rice Noodles 26

One Pot Easy Cheesy Vegetables and Rice 28

One Skillet Pork Supper 29

One Pan Cheesy Chicken and Vegetables 29

Ultimate All in One Chicken Dinner 30

Chicken in a Pot 31

Turkey Pot Pie 32

One Dish Broccoli Rotini 33

Low-Fat Chicken Pot Pie 34

Chicken Pot Pie 36

Chicken Pot Pie 37

Kal Pot	38
Gram's Chicken Pot Pie	39
Chicken or Turkey Pot Pie	40
Cola Pot Roast	41
Clay Pot Meatloaf and Potatoes	42
Chicken Pot Pie	43
Italian Style Pot Roast	44
Oyster Stew for One or Two	45
Kae's Turkey Pot Pie	46
Mini Chicken Pot Pies	48
Pot Roast in Foil	49
Pot Roast with Vegetables	50
One Oh One Cookies	52
Denise Salad Number One	52
One Cup Salad	53
Easy One-Pan Taco Skillet	54
Apple Flavored Pot Roast	55
Oven Bag Pot Roast	56
Pot Roast Caribe	57
Cola Pot Roast	58
Mother's Pot Roast	59
Chicken Pot Pie Casserole	60
Campfire Chicken Pot Pie	61
Fast and Easy Turkey Pot Pie	62
One-Dish Beef Stroganoff and Noodles	63
Simple, Classic Chicken Potpie	64
Best Braised Balsamic Pot Roast	65
Easy Pressure Cooker Pot Roast	66
Healthier Chicken a la King	67
Easy Vegetable Pot Pie	68
Shearers' Mince and Potato Hot Pot	69
Pumpkin Pot De Creme	70
Awesome Slow Cooker Pot Roast Plus Extras	72

Hamburger Pot Pie	73
Three-Pepper Rice and Chicken Pot	74
Impossibly Easy Chicken Pot Pie	75
2-Step Inside-Out Chicken Pot Pie	76
Marie-Eve's Turkey Pot Pie	77
"Black Friday" Turkey Pot Pie	78
All-Natural Chicken Pot Pie	79
Roasted Portobello, Red Pepper, and Arugula Salad for One	81
Pot Roast, Vegetables, and Beer	83
Easy Chicken Pot Pie	84
Mahi Mahi Pot Pie	85
Speedy Chili Pot Pie	86
Angela's Amazing Chicken Pot Pie	87
Stovetop Yankee Pot Roast	89
Cranberry Pot Roast	90
Rustic Chicken Pot Pie	91
Pheasant Pot Pie	92
Kitchen Easy Chicken Pot Pie	94
One - Two - Three - Mexican Macaroni Salad	95
Slow Cooker Au Jus Pot Roast	96
Never Fail Applesauce Spice Cake	97
Slow Cooker Sweet-and-Sour Pot Roast	98
Oven Stew	99
Smoked Sausage Skillet Pot Pie	100
Auto Parts Chicken	101
Easy Weeknight Tuna Pot Pie	102
Grandma Earhart's Pepper Pot Casserole	103
Slow Cooker Savory Pot Roast	104
Mashed Potato-Topped Turkey Pot Pie	105
Apple Cider Pepper Pot Roast (Pressure Cooker Recipe)	106
Puff Pastry Roast Beef Pot Pies	107
Cyndee's Best Slow Cooker Italian Pot Roast	109
To-Die-For Chicken Pot Pie	110

- Chicken and Biscuit Casserole 111
- Healthier (but still awesome) Awesome Slow Cooker Pot Roast 112
- Easy Peach Crisp 113
- Turkey Spaghetti Zoodles 114
- Zucchini Noodle Primavera 115
- Chicken and Rice with Cumin and Cilantro 116
- Chocolate Tahini Pudding 117
- Taiwanese Ground Pork and Pickled Cucumbers 118
- Boeuf Bourguignon 119
- Coconut Red Lentil Curry 120
- Vanilla Sesame Cake 122
- Chicken Stuff 123
- Spicy Spanish Sausage Supper 124
- Pakistani Pot Roast Beef Fillets (Pasanday) 125
- Slow Cooker Chicken Pot Pie Stew 126
- "Eat Them Right Out of the Pot" Vegetarian Collard Greens 127
- Smothered Chicken Breasts 128
- Easy Classic Goulash 129
- Chance's Chicken Spezzatino 130
- Peach Pork Picante 131
- Sweet and Sour Chicken 132
- Authentic Thai Basil Chicken (Very Easy and Fast) 133
- Bo Kho (Spicy Vietnamese Beef Stew) 134
- White Chicken Chili with Rice 135
- Brussels Sprouts 'n Gnocchi 136
- Chili Lime Chicken Tacos 137
- Mama's Old-Fashioned Albondigas (Meatball Soup) 138
- Cilantro Chicken and Rice 140
- Spicy Chicken and Hominy Mexican Soup 141
- Crema di Cavolo Romanesco (Romanesco Broccoli Soup) 142
- Spicy Cayenne Tomato Jam 143
- Zucchini Fenchel Suppe (Zucchini and Fennel Soup) 144
- Kickin' Vegetarian Collard Greens 145

Caribbean Dream Chili 146

Artichoke and Chicken Sausage Cauliflower "Paella" 147

Portuguese Shrimp 148

Portuguese Sopas 149

Osso Bucco-Style Beef Shank 150

Grandmum's Fish Ball Soup 151

Chinese Stir-Fried Sticky Rice with Chinese Sausage 153

Bacon Cider Chili 154

Jessica's Vegetarian Chili 156

Cheesy Sausage Lasagna Soup 157

Chicken Pasta with Artichoke Hearts 158

Pan-Roasted Red Potatoes 159

Easy Lime Cilantro Rice 160

Skillet Chicken Picante 161

One Pot Pasta

Servings: 4

Yield: 4 servings

Ingredients

- 1 teaspoon olive oil
- ½ cup sliced onion
- 1 cup fresh sliced mushrooms
- 1 (29 ounce) can diced tomatoes
- 1 (8 ounce) can tomato sauce
- 1 cup water
- 2 teaspoons dried basil
- 1 teaspoon dried oregano
- 1 teaspoon white sugar
- ¼ teaspoon garlic powder
- ¼ teaspoon ground black pepper
- 8 ounces macaroni

Directions

Step 1

Spray a large nonstick skillet with nonstick cooking spray. Add oil, and heat over a medium flame. Add onion and mushrooms. Cook, stirring frequently, for 3 to 5 minutes, until tender.

Step 2

Add tomatoes, tomato sauce, water, sugar, and spices to skillet. When mixture begins to boil, stir in pasta. Cover, reduce heat to medium-low, and cook 20 minutes. Stir mixture every 4 to 5 minutes while cooking.

Nutrition Facts

Per Serving:

290.1 calories; protein 10.6g 21% DV; carbohydrates 55.2g 18% DV; fat 2.3g 4% DV; cholesterolmg; sodium 775.2mg 31% DV.

One-Pot Mediterranean Chicken

Prep: 15 mins **Cook:** 30 mins **Total:** 45 mins

Servings: 6

Yield: 6 servings

Ingredients

- 1 stick butter
- ½ cup chopped onions
- 1 tablespoon minced garlic
- 1 teaspoon Italian seasoning
- ½ teaspoon dried basil
- salt to taste
- 2 (14 ounce) cans artichoke hearts, drained and quartered
- 1 (28 ounce) can crushed tomatoes
- 1 (14.5 ounce) can diced tomatoes
- 1 (6 ounce) can black olives, halved
- 1 (4.5 ounce) can sliced mushrooms, drained
- 4 eaches boneless, skinless chicken breasts

Directions

Step 1

Melt butter in a large skillet over medium-high heat. Add onions, garlic, Italian seasoning, basil, and salt. Saute until it starts to brown, about 5 minutes.

Step 2

Add artichoke hearts, crushed tomatoes, diced tomatoes, olives, and mushrooms; bring to a boil. Add chicken, cover, and reduce heat to medium. Cook, stirring occasionally, until chicken is cooked through and the juices run clear, about 20 to 25 minutes.

Cook's Notes:

Chicken tenderloins can be used instead of chicken breasts.

Oregano can be used in place of Italian seasoning.

You can leave this over low heat for an hour or so if needed, though the chicken may fall apart.

Nutrition Facts

Per Serving:

360.7 calories; protein 20.3g 41% DV; carbohydrates 23.5g 8% DV; fat 20.6g 32% DV; cholesterol 79.7mg 27% DV; sodium 1400.6mg 56% DV.

One-Pot Pizza Tortellini Bake

Prep: 5 mins **Cook:** 30 mins **Total:** 35 mins

Servings: 8

Yield: 8 servings

Ingredients

nonstick cooking spray

- 1 pound frozen cheese tortellini
- 1 (28 ounce) jar pasta sauce
- ½ cup water
- 1 (14.5 ounce) can diced tomatoes
- 2 cups shredded mozzarella cheese
- 21 slices pepperoni

Directions

Step 1

Preheat the oven to 425 degrees F (220 degrees C). Spray a large, oven-safe, round skillet with cooking spray.

Step 2

Place frozen tortellini in the prepared skillet. Cover with sauce, water, and diced tomatoes; no need to stir. Cover with mozzarella cheese and arrange pepperonis on top.

Step 3

Bake in the preheated oven until cheese is browned, about 30 minutes.

Cook's Note:

You can use pizza sauce instead of pasta sauce, if preferred.

Nutrition Facts

Per Serving:

382.8 calories; protein 18.6g 37% DV; carbohydrates 42.2g 14% DV; fat 15.2g 23% DV; cholesterol 48.1mg 16% DV; sodium 993.2mg 40% DV.

One-Pot Shrimp Scampi Orzo

Prep: 10 mins **Cook:** 20 mins **Additional:** 15 mins **Total:** 45 mins

Servings: 2

Yield: 2 servings

Ingredients

Marinade:

- 1 tablespoon olive oil
- 1 teaspoon lemon zest
- 1 teaspoon lemon juice
- 1 pinch red pepper flakes
- ½ teaspoon dried parsley
- ½ pound uncooked medium shrimp, peeled and deveined
- 1 tablespoon butter
- 1 tablespoon olive oil
- ¾ cup orzo
- ½ cup finely diced onion
- 1 large clove garlic, minced
- ¼ cup white wine
- 1 ¼ cups low-sodium chicken broth
- ½ teaspoon salt
- ½ teaspoon freshly ground black pepper
- ½ cup frozen peas, defrosted
- ½ tablespoon chopped fresh parsley
- 2 slice (1/4" thick) (blank)s lemon slices

Directions

Step 1

Combine olive oil, lemon zest, lemon juice, red pepper flakes, and dried parsley in a small bowl. Add shrimp and toss to coat. Marinate for 15 to 20 minutes.

Step 2

Melt butter in a pot over medium-high heat. Add olive oil. Stir in orzo and onion, toss to coat, and cook, stirring frequently, until onions are translucent and orzo is lightly toasted, 4 to 5 minutes. Mix in garlic and cook until fragrant, about 30 seconds.

Step 3

Deglaze pot with white wine and stir until wine has cooked off. Pour in chicken broth and season with salt and pepper. Cook, stirring frequently, until orzo is tender yet firm to the bite, 8 to 10 minutes. Add peas and shrimp with marinade to the pot, cover, and cook, stirring occasionally, until shrimp are light pink, 3 to 4 minutes.

Step 4

Divide between 2 dishes, sprinkle with fresh parsley, and garnish with lemon slices.

Nutrition Facts

Per Serving:

625.2 calories; protein 33.7g 68% DV; carbohydrates 69.5g 22% DV; fat 21.9g 34% DV; cholesterol 190.4mg 64% DV; sodium 942.7mg 38% DV.

One Pot Tuna Casserole

Prep: 10 mins **Cook:** 20 mins **Total:** 30 mins

Servings: 8

Yield: 8 servings

Ingredients

- 1 (16 ounce) package egg noodles
- 1 (10 ounce) package frozen green peas, thawed
- ¼ cup butter
- 1 (10.75 ounce) can condensed cream of mushroom soup
- 1 (5 ounce) can tuna, drained
- ¼ cup milk
- 1 cup shredded Cheddar cheese

Directions

Step 1

Bring a large pot of lightly salted water to a boil. Cook pasta in boiling water until al dente, adding peas for the final 3 minutes of cooking; drain.

Step 2

Melt the butter in the same pot over medium heat. Add the mushroom soup, tuna, milk, and Cheddar cheese. Stir until cheese is melted, and the mixture is smooth. Stir in the pasta and peas until evenly coated.

Cook's Note:

You can use cream of celery soup instead of the cream of mushroom, if you prefer.

Nutrition Facts

Per Serving:

395.4 calories; protein 17.4g 35% DV; carbohydrates 43.2g 14% DV; fat 17g 26% DV; cholesterol 79.3mg 26% DV; sodium 451.6mg 18% DV.

Spicy One-Pot Shakshouka

Prep: 20 mins **Cook:** 15 mins **Total:** 35 mins

Servings: 4

Yield: 4 servings

Ingredients

- 2 tablespoons olive oil
- 1 onion, halved and finely chopped
- 1 green bell pepper, finely chopped
- 1 red bell pepper, finely chopped
- 1 red chile pepper, seeded and finely chopped
- 2 cloves garlic, minced
- 1 (14 ounce) can diced tomatoes
- 1 teaspoon white sugar
- salt and freshly ground black pepper to taste
- 4 large eggs
- 2 eaches green onions, finely chopped

Directions

Step 1

Heat olive oil in a heavy-bottomed frying pan. Saute onion and bell peppers in the hot oil for 2 to 3 minutes. Add chile pepper and garlic; cook and stir the peppers start to caramelize, 2 to 3 minutes. Add tomatoes and sugar. Cook over medium heat for 3 to 4 minutes. Season with salt and pepper.

Step 2

Make indentations in the sauce using a wooden spoon. Crack eggs into indentations in the sauce. Cover and cook until whites are firm and yolks reach desired doneness, 5 to 8 minutes. Uncover and garnish with green onions.

Nutrition Facts

Per Serving:

202.7 calories; protein 8.7g 18% DV; carbohydrates 15.2g 5% DV; fat 12g 18% DV; cholesterol 186mg 62% DV; sodium 271.5mg 11% DV.

One-Pot Breakfast

Prep: 15 mins **Cook:** 25 mins **Total:** 40 mins

Servings: 10

Yield: 10 servings

Ingredients

- 1 pound bacon, cut into 1/2-inch pieces
- 2 medium onions, diced
- 2 eaches green bell peppers, diced
- 14 eaches eggs
- 1 (26 ounce) package shredded hash brown potatoes
- 1 tablespoon kosher salt
- 1 tablespoon coarsely ground black pepper
- 1 tablespoon garlic powder
- 1 (12 ounce) package shredded Cheddar cheese

Directions

Step 1

Heat a large, heavy-bottomed stainless steel pot over medium heat. Cook bacon until dark brown and crispy, about 8 minutes. Add onions and bell peppers and cook until just starting to soften, about 5 minutes.

Step 2

Crack eggs into the pot; stir to break the yolks and mix eggs evenly. Heat until mostly set but still creamy, about 5 minutes. Add potatoes; toss until evenly distributed. Cook, stirring frequently and scraping the bottom, until potatoes are tender yet firm to the bite, 5 to 7 minutes. Season with salt, pepper, and garlic powder. Remove from heat and add Cheddar cheese; mix until melted.

Cook's Note:

This recipe is good for 12 to 18 eggs and 24 to 30 ounces of potatoes.

Nutrition Facts

Per Serving:

381.2 calories; protein 23.8g 48% DV; carbohydrates 18.4g 6% DV; fat 28.1g 43% DV; cholesterol 280.8mg 94% DV; sodium 1240.6mg 50% DV.

Thai Style One-Pot

Prep: 10 mins **Cook:** 30 mins **Additional:** 5 mins **Total:** 45 mins

Servings: 4

Yield: 4 servings

Ingredients

- 2 teaspoons vegetable oil
- 1 pound ground pork
- 2 eaches red bell peppers, cut into strips
- 2 cups chicken broth
- 1 cup uncooked white rice
- 1 tablespoon soy sauce
- ¾ tablespoon chile-garlic sauce
- 4 ounces snow peas, trimmed and halved
- 4 eaches scallions, thinly sliced
- ½ cup coarsely chopped fresh cilantro
- 2 tablespoons lime juice

Directions

Step 1

Heat oil in a large saucepan over medium heat. Add pork and cook until browned, 7 to 10 minutes. Drain and discard grease.

Step 2

Add peppers to the saucepan with the pork. Cook until starting to soften, about 3 minutes. Stir in broth, rice, soy sauce, and chile-garlic sauce and bring to a boil. Reduce heat and simmer until rice is tender, about 20 minutes.

Step 3

Remove saucepan from heat. Stir in snow peas, scallions, cilantro, and lime juice. Let stand 5 minutes.

Nutrition Facts

Per Serving:

472.2 calories; protein 26.1g 52% DV; carbohydrates 45.8g 15% DV; fat 19.4g 30% DV; cholesterol 76.6mg 26% DV; sodium 994.5mg 40% DV.

One-Pot Ham and Veggie Pasta

Prep: 15 mins **Cook:** 30 mins **Total:** 45 mins

Servings: 6

Yield: 6 servings

Ingredients

- 1 tablespoon olive oil
- 2 ½ cups cubed fully cooked ham
- ½ cup chopped onion
- 3 cloves garlic, minced
- 1 teaspoon Italian seasoning
- ¼ teaspoon red pepper flakes
- salt and pepper to taste
- chopped parsley for garnish
- 4 cups low-sodium chicken broth
- 1 ¼ cups fat free half-and-half
- ¼ cup all-purpose flour
- 1 (16 ounce) package farfalle (bow tie) pasta
- 2 cups frozen peas and carrots
- ½ cup grated Parmesan cheese

Directions

Step 1

Heat olive oil in a large pot over medium heat. Add ham and onion; saute for about 3 minutes. Add garlic and cook until fragrant, about 30 seconds. Stir in Italian seasoning, red pepper flakes, salt and pepper; cook for 2 minutes.

Step 2

Whisk together chicken broth, half-and-half, and flour in a bowl until smooth; pour into the pot. Stir in farfalle pasta, cover, and cook for 15 minutes.

Step 3

Add peas and carrots. Cook until pasta is cooked through, about 8 more minutes. Stir in Parmesan cheese and garnish with chopped parsley. Serve immediately.

Cook's Note:

If the consistency is too thick, add a bit more chicken broth. You can change up this recipe by using a different shape pasta or switching out the Parmesan cheese for another type of cheese.

Nutrition Facts

Per Serving:

552.1 calories; protein 28.9g 58% DV; carbohydrates 71.3g 23% DV; fat 17.6g 27% DV; cholesterol 42.6mg 14% DV; sodium 1042mg 42% DV.

Vegan One-Pot Coconut Curry with Pasta and Vegetables

Prep: 10 mins **Cook:** 20 mins **Total:** 30 mins

Servings: 6

Yield: 6 servings

Ingredients

- 2 tablespoons olive oil
- 1 onion, chopped
- 2 cloves garlic, minced
- 1 pound rigatoni pasta
- 1 (14 ounce) can full-fat coconut milk
- 1 (14.5 ounce) can petite diced tomatoes
- 1 cup water
- ½ (15 ounce) can garbanzo beans, drained
- 3 teaspoons red curry paste
- 2 teaspoons curry powder, or more to taste
- ½ teaspoon garlic powder
- salt and freshly ground black pepper to taste
- ground red pepper to taste
- 2 cups cherry tomatoes, halved
- 3 cups fresh spinach

Directions

Step 1

Heat olive oil in a large saucepan over medium heat and cook onion until soft and translucent, about 3 minutes. Add garlic and cook 1 more minute. Add rigatoni pasta, coconut milk, diced tomatoes, water, garbanzo beans, red curry paste, curry powder, garlic powder, salt, black pepper, and red pepper; stir to combine. Cover with a tight-fitting lid and bring to a boil. Reduce heat and simmer, stirring every 2 minutes, for 13 to 15 minutes.

Step 2

Stir in cherry tomatoes and spinach; cook for 2 to 3 more minutes. Taste and adjust seasoning with salt, black pepper, and red pepper.

Nutrition Facts

Per Serving:

511.1 calories; protein 14.4g 29% DV; carbohydrates 70.7g 23% DV; fat 20.8g 32% DV; cholesterolmg; sodium 282.1mg 11% DV.

Quick One-Pot Chicken Alfredo

Prep: 10 mins **Cook:** 20 mins **Total:** 30 mins

Servings: 4

Yield: 4 servings

Ingredients

- ½ pound skinless, boneless chicken breasts
- ½ teaspoon garlic salt
- ½ teaspoon Italian seasoning
- 1 tablespoon olive oil
- 2 cups milk
- 1 large clove garlic, minced
- 8 ounces fettucine, broken in half
- ½ cup heavy whipping cream
- ¾ cup freshly grated Parmesan cheese, plus more for serving

Directions

Step 1

Slice each chicken breast horizontally into 3 thinner pieces using a sharp knife. Sprinkle each chicken piece with garlic salt and Italian seasoning on both sides.

Step 2

Heat olive oil in a large skillet over medium-high heat. Add chicken and cook until golden and cooked through, about 2 minutes per side. Remove onto a plate.

Step 3

Add milk and garlic to the skillet. Bring to a simmer and add fettuccine. Cook, stirring every 30 seconds to prevent sticking until pasta has softened, about 3 minutes. Reduce heat to medium and cook, stirring every couple of minutes, 6 to 7 minutes more. Stir in cream and Parmesan cheese. Simmer, stirring occasionally, until sauce has thickened and pasta is cooked, about 2 more minutes.

Step 4

Serve immediately and garnish with additional Parmesan cheese if desired.

Nutrition Facts

Per Serving:

532.6 calories; protein 30.7g 61% DV; carbohydrates 48.7g 16% DV; fat 24.2g 37% DV; cholesterol 98.3mg 33% DV; sodium 550.4mg 22% DV.

One-Pot Spaghetti with Meat Sauce

Prep: 10 mins **Cook:** 30 mins **Total:** 40 mins

Servings: 4

Yield: 4 servings

Ingredients

- 1 pound ground Italian sausage
- 1 small white onion, diced
- 4 cloves garlic, minced
- 2 cups water
- 1 (26 ounce) jar tomato-basil pasta sauce
- 1 teaspoon Italian seasoning
- 1 (8 ounce) package spaghetti noodles, broken in half
- ½ cup freshly grated Parmesan cheese for serving

Directions

Step 1

Combine ground sausage, onions, and garlic in a large pot or skillet with tall sides. Cook over medium heat until sausage is cooked through, 5 to 8 minutes. Drain and discard grease.

Step 2

Stir water, pasta sauce, and Italian seasoning into the pot; bring to a boil. Stir in spaghetti noodles, return to a boil and cook, stirring occasionally, until noodles are cooked through and sauce has thickened, 17 to 20 minutes.

Step 3

Serve topped with grated Parmesan cheese.

Cook's Note:

You can use mild or medium spiced ground Italian sausage.

Nutrition Facts

Per Serving:

606.4 calories; protein 29.5g 59% DV; carbohydrates 66.1g 21% DV; fat 26.6g 41% DV; cholesterol 53.4mg 18% DV; sodium 1650.9mg 66% DV.

One-Pot Moroccan Shrimp Tagine

Prep: 20 mins **Cook:** 35 mins **Total:** 55 mins

Servings: 6

Yield: 6 servings

Ingredients

- 3 tablespoons olive oil
- 4 large carrots, chopped
- 1 large sweet onion, diced
- 1 large russet potato, peeled and diced
- 1 red bell pepper, thinly sliced
- ½ cup pitted Kalamata olives, sliced
- 2 tablespoons minced garlic
- 2 teaspoons ginger paste
- 2 large tomatoes, coarsely chopped
- ½ cup chopped fresh cilantro
- 1 tablespoon dried parsley
- 2 teaspoons ground cumin
- 2 teaspoons seasoned salt
- 1 (1.41 ounce) package sazon seasoning with saffron (such as Goya Azafran)
- 1 teaspoon paprika
- 1 teaspoon ground turmeric
- 1 teaspoon lemon juice
- ½ teaspoon cayenne pepper
- ½ teaspoon ground black pepper
- 1 bay leaf
- 1 pound uncooked medium shrimp, peeled and deveined

Directions

Step 1

Heat a Dutch oven over medium-high heat. Add olive oil. Saute carrots, onion, potato, and bell pepper until soft, about 5 minutes. Add olives, garlic, and ginger paste and saute for 2 minutes.

Step 2

Stir in tomatoes, cilantro, parsley, cumin, seasoned salt, sazon, paprika, turmeric, lemon juice, cayenne, black pepper, and bay leaf. Cover and cook until tomatoes have broken down and flavors have combined, about 20 minutes. Add shrimp, cover, and cook until they are bright pink, about 5 minutes.

Nutrition Facts

Per Serving:

274.9 calories; protein 16.3g 33% DV; carbohydrates 28.8g 9% DV; fat 11.2g 17% DV; cholesterol 115mg 38% DV; sodium 1669.8mg 67% DV.

One-Pot White Chicken Chili

Prep: 10 mins **Cook:** 1 hr 30 mins **Total:** 1 hr 40 mins

Servings: 8

Yield: 8 servings

Ingredients

- 1 tablespoon olive oil, or to taste
- 2 large skinless, boneless chicken breasts, cut into bite-size pieces
- 2 cloves garlic, chopped
- 1 tablespoon dried chives
- 1 tablespoon dried oregano
- 1 tablespoon dried thyme
- 1 tablespoon dried basil
- salt and ground black pepper to taste
- 1 bay leaf
- 5 (14.5 ounce) cans great Northern beans, divided
- 14 ½ fluid ounces water
- 1 (14.5 ounce) can chopped tomatoes
- 1 (12 ounce) jar salsa
- 1 cup sour cream

Directions

Step 1

Heat olive oil in a large pot over medium heat. Add chicken, garlic, chives, oregano, thyme, basil, salt, pepper, and bay leaf; cook and stir until juices run clear, 5 to 8 minutes. Stir in 3 cans great Northern beans, water, chopped tomatoes, and salsa. Reduce heat to low and simmer, stirring occasionally, until flavors combine, about 1 hour.

Step 2

Stir remaining 2 cans great Northern beans and sour cream into the pot. Increase heat to medium-low and simmer until thick, about 25 minutes. Ladle into bowls.

Nutrition Facts

Per Serving:

450.4 calories; protein 31.9g 64% DV; carbohydrates 60g 19% DV; fat 10g 15% DV; cholesterol 41.9mg 14% DV; sodium 402.7mg 16% DV.

One-Pot Rice and Beef Pilaf

Prep: 20 mins **Cook:** 1 hr 15 mins **Total:** 1 hr 35 mins

Servings: 4

Yield: 4 servings

Ingredients

- ½ cup olive oil
- 2 cups uncooked white rice
- 2 pounds bone-in beef pot roast, boned and cubed
- 1 onion, peeled, halved, and thinly sliced
- salt to taste
- hot water to cover
- 4 carrot, (7-1/2")s carrots, peeled and cut into matchsticks
- 2 teaspoons ground cumin
- 2 peppers fresh red chile peppers
- 1 head garlic, unpeeled

Directions

Step 1

Place rice in a bowl, cover with warm water, and soak while meat is cooking.

Step 2

Heat olive oil in a pot over medium-high heat and saute bones until lightly browned, about 5 minutes. Transfer bones to a plate. Add onion to the same pot and cook until soft and translucent, about 5 minutes. Add beef and brown on all sides, 5 to 10 minutes.

Step 3

Return bones to the pan and stir in carrots. Sprinkle with cumin. Add whole chile peppers and garlic; stir everything together and season with salt. Pour in enough hot water to cover. Bring to a boil, reduce heat and simmer until flavors are well combined, 35 to 40 minutes.

Step 4

Remove bones with kitchen tongs and add rice. Pour in 2 cups hot water and smooth the rice out so it lays flat on the top, but do not stir. Cover pot and cook over low heat until rice is soft, 20 to 25 minutes. Stir together before serving.

Nutrition Facts

Per Serving:

988.2 calories; protein 35.6g 71% DV; carbohydrates 90.5g 29% DV; fat 53.1g 82% DV; cholesterol 103mg 34% DV; sodium 172.3mg 7% DV.

Easy One-Pot Chicken Alfredo

Prep: 10 mins **Cook:** 20 mins **Total:** 30 mins

Servings: 6

Yield: 6 servings

Ingredients

- 2 tablespoons vegetable oil
- 2 eaches boneless, skinless chicken breasts, cut into 1-inch cubes
- 1 large onion, diced
- 4 cloves garlic, minced
- ½ teaspoon salt
- ½ teaspoon ground black pepper
- 2 tablespoons all-purpose flour
- 3 cups low-sodium chicken broth
- 2 cups unsweetened almond milk
- 1 teaspoon dried basil
- ¾ teaspoon dried oregano
- 1 pinch ground nutmeg
- 16 ounces tricolor rotini pasta
- 1 cup grated Parmigiano-Reggiano cheese, or more to taste
- ¼ cup Greek yogurt

Directions

Step 1

Heat vegetable oil in a large pot over medium heat. Add chicken, onion, and garlic. Season with salt and black pepper, and cook until lightly browned and chicken is no longer pink, 5 to 7 minutes. Sprinkle flour over chicken. Stir and cook for 1 minute. Pour in chicken broth and almond milk. Season with basil, oregano, and nutmeg. Stir to combine.

Step 2

Mix in rotini pasta and bring mixture to a boil over medium-high heat. Cover, reduce heat to low, and cook until sauce is slightly thickened and pasta is cooked, about 10 minutes, stirring occasionally.

Step 3

Remove from heat and stir in Parmesan cheese and Greek yogurt. Season with additional salt and black pepper to taste. Mixture will thicken as it cools. Serve topped with additional Parmesan cheese, if desired.

Nutrition Facts

Per Serving:

489.2 calories; protein 26.6g 53% DV; carbohydrates 65.4g 21% DV; fat 12.8g 20% DV; cholesterol 38.7mg 13% DV; sodium 538.8mg 22% DV.

One-Pot Spinach Mushroom Lasagna

Servings: 12

Yield: 12 servings

Ingredients

- 1 tablespoon olive oil
- 8 ounces baby bella (crimini) mushrooms, chopped
- 1 teaspoon crushed red pepper flakes, or to taste
- 5 ounces fresh baby spinach, chopped
- 1 (24 ounce) jar Ragu Old World Style Traditional Sauce
- 3 cups water
- 12 noodles uncooked lasagna noodles, broken into 2-inch pieces
- 1 ¼ cups part-skim ricotta cheese
- ¾ cup shredded part-skim mozzarella cheese
- 1 teaspoon Grated Parmesan cheese for garnish

Directions

Step 1

Heat oil in a large skillet over medium-high heat. Add mushrooms and cook until softened, about 5 minutes. Add red pepper flakes and spinach, cooking until spinach is wilted.

Step 2

Stir in Ragu Sauce and water. Bring to a boil. Stir in uncooked noodles. Reduce heat to medium and cook covered until noodles are tender, about 20 minutes. Note: be sure to stir frequently so the noodles do not settle at the bottom of the pan.

Step 3

Top noodles with spoonfuls of ricotta cheese and then sprinkle with mozzarella cheese. Reduce heat to a simmer and cook covered until cheese is melted (about 5 minutes). Sprinkle with grated Parmesan cheese, if desired.

Nutrition Facts

Per Serving:

160.4 calories; protein 7g 14% DV; carbohydrates 24.3g 8% DV; fat 4.1g 6% DV; cholesterol 4.7mg 2% DV; sodium 409mg 16% DV.

One-Pot Lebanese Chicken and Rice

Prep: 10 mins **Cook:** 40 mins **Total:** 50 mins

Servings: 4

Yield: 4 servings

Ingredients

- 3 tablespoons olive oil
- 4 eaches skinless, boneless chicken breasts
- 4 ounces diced onion
- 12 ounces ground beef
- 1 tablespoon minced garlic
- 2 teaspoons ground cinnamon
- 1 teaspoon ground allspice
- ¾ teaspoon salt
- ¼ teaspoon ground cayenne pepper
- 1 ½ cups long grain rice
- 3 cups chicken broth
- 2 tablespoons chopped fresh parsley

Directions

Step 1

Preheat the oven to 375 degrees F (190 degrees C).

Step 2

Heat olive oil in a heavy, oven-safe skillet over high heat. Cook chicken breasts on both sides until golden brown, about 5 minutes per side. Remove chicken breasts from skillet and set aside. Add onion and ground beef to the skillet; cook until onions are starting to brown, about 5 minutes. Add garlic and cook for 1 to 2 minutes. Season with cinnamon, allspice, salt, and cayenne pepper. Cook and stir for 2 minutes.

Step 3

Stir rice into the skillet until fully coated with oil and spices. Place chicken breasts on top of the rice and pour in broth. Cover skillet with a tight-fitting lid or aluminum foil.

Step 4

Bake in the preheated oven until rice has absorbed all liquid, about 20 minutes. Remove from oven and sprinkle with parsley before serving.

Cook's Note:

A cast-iron skillet works best for this dish. You can also use ground lamb instead of beef.

Nutrition Facts

Per Serving:

680.2 calories; protein 44g 88% DV; carbohydrates 61.1g 20% DV; fat 27.1g 42% DV; cholesterol 121.2mg 40% DV; sodium 1420.8mg 57% DV.

One-Pot Cajun Chicken and Sausage Alfredo Pasta

Prep: 15 mins **Cook:** 35 mins **Total:** 50 mins

Servings: 6

Yield: 6 servings

Ingredients

- 1 pound chicken, cut into bite-sized pieces
- ½ teaspoon kosher salt
- freshly ground black pepper to taste
- 4 tablespoons extra-virgin olive oil
- 14 ounces smoked sausage, sliced on the diagonal
- 4 cloves garlic, minced

- 2 cups low-sodium chicken broth
- 1 ¼ cups heavy cream
- 2 cups dried penne pasta
- 1 ½ tablespoons Cajun seasoning, plus more to taste
- ½ cup freshly shredded Parmesan cheese
- 1 tablespoon minced Italian flat-leaf parsley

Directions

Step 1

Season chicken with salt and pepper. Heat olive oil in a large, covered cooking pot over medium-high heat. Brown chicken in the hot oil, 5 to 7 minutes.

Step 2

Add sausage to the pot and continue to cook until lightly browned, about 5 minutes more. Stir in garlic and cook for about 2 minutes. Add chicken broth, heavy cream, pasta, and Cajun seasoning. Stir together and bring to a simmer over medium-high heat, about 5 minutes.

Step 3

Reduce heat to low, cover the pot, and cook until pasta is tender, 15 to 20 minutes.

Step 4

Remove the pot from heat and stir in Parmesan cheese. Stir in chopped parsley and sprinkle with additional Cajun seasoning if desired.

Nutrition Facts

Per Serving:

723.1 calories; protein 38.6g 77% DV; carbohydrates 22.4g 7% DV; fat 52.9g 81% DV; cholesterol 163.2mg 54% DV; sodium 1706.5mg 68% DV.

One-Pot Chicken Enchilada Mac and Cheese

Prep: 10 mins **Cook:** 30 mins **Total:** 40 mins

Servings: 8

Yield: 8 servings

Ingredients

- 16 ounces elbow macaroni
- 1 (10 ounce) can red enchilada sauce
- 1 cup half-and-half
- 1 (4 ounce) can chopped green chilies
- 2 cups shredded sharp Cheddar cheese
- 2 cups shredded pepperjack cheese
- 2 cups cubed cooked chicken
- ¼ cup chopped cilantro

Directions

Step 1

Bring a large pot of lightly salted water to a boil. Cook elbow macaroni in the boiling water, stirring occasionally, until tender yet firm to the bite, about 8 minutes. Drain and set aside.

Step 2

Combine enchilada sauce, half-and-half, and green chiles in the same pot over medium heat and cook until warm, 5 to 10 minutes. Slowly add Cheddar cheese and pepperjack cheese and whisk continuously until melted, about 5 minutes. Return cooked macaroni to the pot. Add chicken and cilantro and stir until combined and heated through, about 5 minutes more.

Cook's Note:

To reheat leftovers, add chicken broth a little at a time until desired consistency is reached.

Nutrition Facts

Per Serving:

582.4 calories; protein 29.8g 60% DV; carbohydrates 47.9g 15% DV; fat 29.7g 46% DV; cholesterol 103.8mg 35% DV; sodium 701mg 28% DV.

One Pot Thai-Style Rice Noodles

Prep: 20 mins **Cook:** 15 mins **Additional:** 5 mins **Total:** 40 mins

Servings: 4

Yield: 4 servings

Ingredients

- 2 tablespoons cornstarch
- 1 ½ tablespoons water
- 6 cups chicken broth
- 2 ½ tablespoons soy sauce

- 1 tablespoon fish sauce
- 1 tablespoon rice vinegar
- 1 tablespoon chile-garlic sauce (such as Sriracha), or more to taste
- 2 teaspoons vegetable oil
- 2 teaspoons minced fresh ginger root
- 2 cloves garlic, minced
- 1 teaspoon ground coriander
- 1 (16 ounce) package thick rice noodles
- 1 cup sliced zucchini
- 1 cup sliced red bell pepper
- 2 breast half, bone and skin removed (blank)s cooked chicken breasts, cut into 1-inch cubes
- ¼ cup crushed peanuts
- ¼ cup chopped fresh cilantro

Directions

Step 1

Stir cornstarch and water together in a small bowl until smooth. Pour chicken broth into a large pot and stir cornstarch mixture, soy sauce, fish sauce, rice vinegar, chile-garlic sauce, vegetable oil, ginger, garlic, and coriander into broth. Cover and bring to a boil.

Step 2

Place rice noodles in the boiling sauce, reduce heat to medium, and simmer until noodles are tender, 5 to 10 minutes. Stir zucchini, red bell pepper, and chicken into sauce. Bring back to a boil, cover, and simmer until vegetables are just become tender, about 5 more minutes.

Step 3

Remove from heat and let stand, covered, for 5 minutes to thicken. Serve garnished with crushed peanuts and cilantro.

Cook's Note:

I often use frozen mixed vegetables in a pinch for an even quicker meal.

Nutrition Facts

Per Serving:

586.8 calories; protein 17.4g 35% DV; carbohydrates 104.9g 34% DV; fat 9.2g 14% DV; cholesterol 29.6mg 10% DV; sodium 2736.3mg 110% DV.

One Pot Easy Cheesy Vegetables and Rice

Prep: 5 mins **Cook:** 10 mins **Total:** 15 mins

Servings: 4

Yield: 4 servings

Ingredients

- 1 ½ tablespoons vegetable or canola oil
- ½ teaspoon Morton Fine Sea Salt
- 1 cup extra long grain rice (15 minute)
- 2 cups frozen mixed vegetables
- 3 cups chicken stock
- 1 ½ cups shredded Cheddar cheese

Directions

Step 1

Heat oil in medium sauce pan over medium-high heat.

Step 2

Add remaining **ingredients**, except for cheese.

Step 3

Bring to a boil for 1 minute.

Step 4

Reduce heat to low, cover and simmer for 10 minutes, or until liquid is absorbed.

Step 5

Add cheese and stir until melted and serve immediately.

Nutrition Facts

Per Serving:

366.3 calories; protein 15.6g 31% DV; carbohydrates 31.8g 10% DV; fat 20.3g 31% DV; cholesterol 45.1mg 15% DV; sodium 1098mg 44% DV.

One Skillet Pork Supper

Servings: 4

Yield: 4 servings

Ingredients

- 4 raw chop with refuse, 151 g; (blank) 5.3 ounces pork chops
- 1 (10.75 ounce) can condensed tomato soup
- ½ cup water
- 1 teaspoon Worcestershire sauce
- ½ teaspoon salt
- 3 medium (2-1/4" to 3" dia, raw)s potatoes, quartered
- 4 small carrots, cut into 2 inch pieces

Directions

Step 1

In a large skillet, brown pork chops over medium heat for about 4 to 6 minutes each side. Pour off fat. Add the tomato soup, water, Worcestershire sauce, salt, potatoes, and carrots. Cover skillet, reduce heat to medium low and let simmer for 45 minutes or until tender.

Nutrition Facts

Per Serving:

317.7 calories; protein 25.3g 51% DV; carbohydrates 43.1g 14% DV; fat 5.2g 8% DV; cholesterol 64.9mg 22% DV; sodium 826.5mg 33% DV.

One Pan Cheesy Chicken and Vegetables

Prep: 10 mins **Cook:** 15 mins **Total:** 25 mins

Servings: 4

Yield: 4 servings

Ingredients

- 1 tablespoon olive oil

- 1 pound skinless, boneless chicken thighs, cut into strips
- 1 medium onion, finely diced
- 2 medium carrots, peeled and diced
- 2 stalks celery, diced
- 1 (5.6 ounce) package Knorr Rice Sides™ - Chicken
- 2 cups water
- 1 ½ teaspoons dried basil
- ¾ cup shredded Cheddar cheese

Directions

Step 1

Heat oil over medium-high heat in a non-stick skillet. Add chicken; cook and stir until cooked through (no longer pink in the center). Transfer chicken to a bowl.

Step 2

Stir diced onion, carrot, and celery into the pan; cook, stirring occasionally until vegetables start to soften, about 5 minutes. Season with salt and pepper. Stir in water and Knorr Rice Sides™ - Chicken flavor. Bring to a simmer over high heat; reduce to medium-low; cover and simmer 7 minutes.

Step 3

Stir in cooked chicken, basil, and shredded Cheddar cheese.

Nutrition Facts

Per Serving:

472 calories; protein 27.4g 55% DV; carbohydrates 16.3g 5% DV; fat 24.8g 38% DV; cholesterol 87.3mg 29% DV; sodium 250.7mg 10% DV.

Ultimate All in One Chicken Dinner

Prep: 15 mins **Cook:** 1 hr **Total:** 1 hr 15 mins

Servings: 4

Yield: 4 servings

Ingredients

- 2 tablespoons vegetable oil
- 2 tablespoons margarine
- 1 medium onion, sliced
- 1 green bell pepper, seeded and cut into strips
- 2 stalks celery, diced

- ¾ cup sliced fresh mushrooms
- 4 breast half, bone and skin removed (blank)s skinless, boneless chicken breast halves
- 4 medium potatoes, peeled and diced
- 2 (14 ounce) cans cut green beans, drained
- 1 (14 ounce) can chicken broth
- 1 teaspoon salt
- ¼ teaspoon dried thyme
- ¼ teaspoon cayenne pepper
- 1 bay leaf

Directions

Step 1

Heat the oil in a skillet over medium heat. Melt the margarine in the skillet. Stir in the onion, bell pepper, celery, and mushrooms, and cook until tender. Set vegetables aside, and cook the chicken breasts in the skillet 10 minutes on each side, until juices run clear.

Step 2

Return the cooked vegetables to the skillet. Mix in the potatoes and green beans. Pour in the chicken broth. Season with salt, thyme, cayenne pepper, and bay leaf. Cover, reduce heat to low, and simmer 30 minutes, stirring occasionally, until potatoes are tender and most of the liquid has been reduced. Remove the bay leaf before serving.

Nutrition Facts

Per Serving:

455.8 calories; protein 30.7g 61% DV; carbohydrates 49.6g 16% DV; fat 15.1g 23% DV; cholesterol 63.3mg 21% DV; sodium 1749.5mg 70% DV.

Chicken in a Pot

Prep: 20 mins **Cook:** 20 mins **Total:** 40 mins

Servings: 4

Yield: 4 servings

Ingredients

- ¾ cup chicken broth
- 1 ½ tablespoons tomato paste
- ¼ teaspoon ground black pepper
- ½ teaspoon dried oregano
- ⅛ teaspoon salt
- 1 clove garlic, minced

- 4 breast half, bone and skin removed (blank)s boneless, skinless chicken breast halves
- 3 tablespoons dry bread crumbs
- 2 teaspoons olive oil
- 2 cups fresh sliced mushrooms

Directions

Step 1

In a medium bowl, combine the broth, tomato paste, ground black pepper, oregano, salt and garlic. Mix well and set aside.

Step 2

Dredge the chicken in the bread crumbs, coating well. Heat the oil in a large skillet over medium high heat. Saute the chicken in the oil for 2 minutes per side, or until lightly browned.

Step 3

Add the reserved broth mixture and the mushrooms to the skillet and bring to a boil. Then cover, reduce heat to low and simmer for 20 minutes. Remove chicken and set aside, covering to keep it warm.

Step 4

Bring broth mixture to a boil and cook for 4 minutes, or until reduced to desired thickness. Spoon sauce over the chicken and serve.

Nutrition Facts

Per Serving:

206 calories; protein 28.7g 57% DV; carbohydrates 6.9g 2% DV; fat 6.6g 10% DV; cholesterol 72.8mg 24% DV; sodium 401.7mg 16% DV.

Turkey Pot Pie

Servings: 7

Yield: 6 to 8 servings

Ingredients

- 1 recipe pastry for a 9 inch double crust pie
- 2 cups cubed cooked turkey
- 2 cups frozen mixed vegetables, thawed
- 2 tablespoons chopped onion
- 1 (10.75 ounce) can condensed cream of chicken soup
- ½ cup milk

Directions

Step 1

Preheat oven to 400 degrees F (200 degrees C). Line bottom of pie pan with crust. In a skillet saute the chopped onion until slightly soft and set aside.

Step 2

Mix together the turkey or chicken, mixed vegetables, onion, soup and milk. Pour into pie crust, cover with top crust and crimp edges.

Step 3

Poke holes in top crust and bake for 40 to 50 minutes.

Nutrition Facts

Per Serving:

422 calories; protein 17.6g 35% DV; carbohydrates 33.9g 11% DV; fat 24.1g 37% DV; cholesterol 37.7mg 13% DV; sodium 608.9mg 24% DV.

One Dish Broccoli Rotini

Prep: 15 mins **Cook:** 15 mins **Total:** 30 mins

Servings: 8

Yield: 8 servings

Ingredients

- 16 ounces fresh broccoli, chopped
- 1 (16 ounce) package rotini pasta
- 2 cloves garlic, minced
- ½ cup olive oil
- ½ cup grated Parmesan cheese
- salt to taste
- ground black pepper to taste

Directions

Step 1

In a large pot, cook broccoli in boiling water until tender. Drain broccoli, but reserve cooking water.

Step 2

Reusing broccoli cooking water, cook rotini pasta until al dente. Drain and remove pasta.

Step 3

In a large pot, saute the garlic in the olive oil. Add the cooked pasta, broccoli, grated Parmesan cheese and toss together. If desired, add salt and pepper to taste.

Nutrition Facts

Per Serving:

361.7 calories; protein 11g 22% DV; carbohydrates 44.9g 15% DV; fat 16.4g 25% DV; cholesterol 4.4mg 2% DV; sodium 98.2mg 4% DV.

Low-Fat Chicken Pot Pie

Prep: 30 mins **Cook:** 1 hr **Total:** 1 hr 30 mins

Servings: 8

Yield: 1 9-inch deep dish pie

Ingredients

- 3 breast half, bone and skin removed (blank)s bone-in chicken breast halves, skinless
- 1 (14.5 ounce) can chicken broth
- 3 medium (2-1/4" to 3" dia, raw)s potatoes
- 1 yellow onion
- 3 stalks celery
- 2 tablespoons vegetable oil
- 2 tablespoons all-purpose flour
- 2 cups frozen mixed vegetables
- 1 to taste salt and pepper to taste
- ¼ teaspoon garlic powder
- 1 (9 inch) frozen prepared pie crust, thawed

Directions

Step 1

Wash chicken breasts in water and then place in a pot with water just to cover the chicken add some salt and pepper and garlic powder. Bring to a boil, turn off heat and cover. Let cool in the pot.

Step 2

Preheat oven to 350 degrees F (175 degrees C).

Step 3

Wash and cut potatoes into bite size pieces and boil till almost fork tender. Drain and set aside.

Step 4

Wash celery and cut to bite-size pieces. Cut onion to bite-size pieces.

Step 5

In a large heavy skillet, over medium heat, saute celery and onion with 2 tablespoons oil, for 5 to 8 minutes. Add the frozen vegetables and cook another 5 minutes. Add flour and cook about 30 seconds.

Step 6

Add chicken broth and bring to a boil. After it has become thick, add potatoes.

Step 7

Remove chicken from pot and cut into bite-size pieces and add to vegetable mixture. Add salt and pepper to taste.

Step 8

Pour mixture into a 9 inch deep dish pie plate and cover with pie shell. Make sure you crimp the edges of the pie shell to the plate so no juices spill in oven.

Step 9

Bake at 350 degrees F (175 degrees C) for 45 minutes or until pie shell is cooked and golden brown.

I Made It Print

Nutrition Facts

Per Serving:

305.9 calories; protein 13.4g 27% DV; carbohydrates 33.6g 11% DV; fat 13.3g 20% DV; cholesterol 26mg 9% DV; sodium 482.6mg 19% DV.

Chicken Pot Pie

Servings: 4

Yield: 4 servings

Ingredients

- 1 ½ pounds skinless, boneless chicken breast meat
- 1 cup chicken broth
- ½ teaspoon salt
- ¼ teaspoon ground black pepper
- 1 ½ cups milk
- 3 tablespoons butter
- 1 onion, chopped
- 1 cup chopped celery
- ⅓ cup all-purpose flour
- 2 cups frozen mixed vegetables, thawed
- 1 tablespoon chopped fresh parsley
- ½ teaspoon dried thyme
- 1 (9 inch) pastry for a 9 inch single crust pie
- 1 egg, lightly beaten

Directions

Step 1

In a large saucepan over medium high heat, combine the chicken meat, chicken broth, salt and pepper. Bring to a boil and reduce heat to low. Cover and let simmer for 30 minutes, or until chicken is no longer pink in the center and the juices run clear.

Step 2

Remove the chicken and let cool. Pour the remaining chicken broth mixture into a measuring cup. Let stand; spoon off fat. Add enough milk to the broth mixture to equal 2 1/2 cups. Cut chicken into 1/2 inch pieces.

Step 3

In the same pan, melt butter or margarine over medium heat. Add the onion and celery. Saute, stirring, for 3 minutes. Stir in flour until well blended. Gradually stir in broth mixture. Simmer, stirring constantly, until the sauce thickens and boils. Add the chicken, vegetables, parsley and thyme. Pour mixture into a 1 1/2 quart deep casserole dish.

Step 4

Preheat oven to 400 degrees F (200 degrees C).

Step 5

Roll out pastry 1 inch larger than the diameter of the casserole dish on a lightly floured surface. Cut slits in the pastry for venting air. Place pastry on top of casserole. Roll edges and cut away extra pastry; flute edges by pinching together. Reroll scraps to cut into decorative designs. Place on top of pastry. Brush pastry with beaten egg and bake in the preheated oven for 30 minutes or until the crust is golden brown and the filling is bubbling. Let cool for 10 minutes and serve.

Nutrition Facts

Per Serving:

665.7 calories; protein 51.4g 103% DV; carbohydrates 47.8g 15% DV; fat 29.5g 45% DV; cholesterol 176.8mg 59% DV; sodium 1055.9mg 42% DV.

Chicken Pot Pie

Prep: 30 mins **Cook:** 25 mins **Total:** 55 mins

Servings: 4

Yield: 4 servings

Ingredients

- 1 cup all-purpose flour
- 2 teaspoons baking powder
- ½ teaspoon ground sage
- ¼ teaspoon salt
- 2 tablespoons butter
- ⅓ cup cold nonfat milk
- 1 cup chopped onions
- 2 cloves garlic
- 1 cup chicken broth
- 1 ½ cups potatoes, peeled and cubed
- 1 ½ cups carrots, chopped
- 1 cup frozen mixed vegetables, thawed
- 1 (10.75 ounce) can reduced fat cream of chicken soup
- 1 ½ tablespoons all-purpose flour
- 2 cups cooked, cubed chicken breast meat
- 2 tablespoons chopped fresh parsley
- ½ teaspoon dried basil
- ½ teaspoon dried thyme
- salt and pepper to taste

Directions

Step 1

Preheat oven to 400 degrees F (200 degrees C).

Step 2

To Make Crust: Mix together 1 cup flour, baking powder, sage, and 1/4 teaspoon salt. Cut in butter or margarine until mixture is crumbly. Stir in milk. Gather dough into a ball, wrap in plastic, and allow to rest in refrigerator.

Step 3

Spray a large nonstick skillet with cooking spray. Cook onions and garlic together over medium heat until soft, about 5 minutes. Add broth, potatoes, carrots, and mixed vegetables. Simmer partially covered for 12 minutes. Potatoes should be slightly undercooked.

Step 4

In a small bowl, combine cream of chicken soup and flour. Mix until smooth. Add mixture to vegetables along with chicken, parsley, basil, thyme, salt, and pepper. Pour mixture into a 2 quart casserole dish.

Step 5

Roll out dough to fit top of casserole dish. Lay dough over filling and prick with a fork several times.

Step 6

Bake in preheated oven for 25 minutes, until crust is golden brown. Allow to sit 5 minutes before serving.

Nutrition Facts

Per Serving:

466.8 calories; protein 33.2g 67% DV; carbohydrates 58.3g 19% DV; fat 11.2g 17% DV; cholesterol 81.8mg 27% DV; sodium 1648.6mg 66% DV.

Kal Pot

Prep: 30 mins **Cook:** 30 mins **Total:** 1 hr

Servings: 5

Yield: 4 to 6 servings

Ingredients

- 2 cups water
- 1 cup uncooked white rice
- 2 pounds boneless pork loin, cut into 1 inch cubes
- 1 onion, chopped
- 4 medium whole (2-3/5" dia) (blank)s tomatoes, cut into bite size pieces
- 2 teaspoons fish sauce
- 1 egg, beaten

Directions

Step 1

In a saucepan bring water to a boil. Add rice and stir. Reduce heat, cover and simmer for 20 minutes.

Step 2

Heat oil in a large skillet or wok. Add pork and onion and stir-fry until done and no pink is showing. Stir in tomatoes and steam until tomatoes are semi-soft. Remove from heat and stir in the cooked rice. Add the fish sauce and beaten egg and stir well; the egg will thicken the mixture. Then it is Kal Pot and ready to serve!

Nutrition Facts

Per Serving:

442.9 calories; protein 34.7g 70% DV; carbohydrates 37.3g 12% DV; fat 16.2g 25% DV; cholesterol 123.3mg 41% DV; sodium 218.5mg 9% DV.

Gram's Chicken Pot Pie

Servings: 6

Yield: 1 - 9 inch pie

Ingredients

- 1 (2 to 3 pound) whole chicken
- 2 (9 inch) deep dish frozen pie crusts, thawed
- 1 (10.75 ounce) can condensed cream of mushroom soup
- 1 (10 ounce) package frozen green peas, thawed
- 2 cups water, or as needed
- 1 teaspoon chicken bouillon granules

Directions

Step 1

In a large heavy pot, place chicken and water to cover. Bring to a boil and let simmer uncovered for 30 minutes, adding water as needed. When chicken is boiled and tender, pick all the meat off of the bones.

Step 2

Preheat oven to 400 degrees F (200 degrees C).

Step 3

Open 1 can of cream of mushroom soup and pour into a small saucepan. Add frozen peas and carrots, water and chicken bouillon to taste. Simmer all together until the soup is smooth. Add chicken meat and mix all together.

Step 4

Pour chicken and soup mixture into one pie crust and cover with the other crust. Seal the edges and cut a small steam hole in the top crust. Bake in the preheated oven 30 to 35 minutes or until crust is brown. Yummy!

Nutrition Facts

Per Serving:

798.2 calories; protein 41.1g 82% DV; carbohydrates 40g 13% DV; fat 51.6g 79% DV; cholesterol 141.9mg 47% DV; sodium 911.2mg 36% DV.

Chicken or Turkey Pot Pie

Prep: 10 mins **Cook:** 40 mins **Total:** 50 mins

Servings: 8

Yield: 8 servings

Ingredients

- 2 eaches prepared pie crusts
- 2 cups coarsely chopped leftover turkey
- 1 (16 ounce) package frozen vegetable blend, thawed
- 1 (10.75 ounce) can condensed cream of chicken soup
- ½ cup half and half, or to taste
- salt and ground black pepper to taste

Directions

Step 1

Preheat oven to 350 degrees F (175 degrees C). Line a pie plate with 1 prepared pie crust.

Step 2

Stir turkey, vegetables, chicken soup, half-and-half, salt, and black pepper together in a bowl. Pour into prepared pie plate and top with remaining pie crust. Slice 4 slits in the top of the crust to vent.

Step 3

Bake in the preheated oven until heated through and crust is golden, 40 to 45 minutes.

Nutrition Facts

Per Serving:

377.3 calories; protein 16.3g 33% DV; carbohydrates 31.5g 10% DV; fat 20.9g 32% DV; cholesterol 35.2mg 12% DV; sodium 560.2mg 22% DV.

Cola Pot Roast

Prep: 15 mins **Cook:** 5 hrs **Total:** 5 hrs 15 mins

Servings: 8

Yield: 8 servings

Ingredients

- 4 pounds beef sirloin roast
- 3 carrot, (7-1/2")s carrots, chopped
- 3 stalks celery, chopped
- 1 clove garlic, minced
- ½ (.75 ounce) packet dry brown gravy mix
- 2 tablespoons water
- 1 (1 ounce) package dry onion soup mix
- 1 (10.75 ounce) can condensed cream of mushroom soup
- 10 fluid ounces cola-flavored carbonated beverage

Directions

Step 1

Preheat oven to 350 degrees F (175 degrees C).

Step 2

Place meat in a roasting pan. Sprinkle carrots, celery and minced garlic around roast.

Step 3

In a small bowl, combine the brown gravy mix and water, mixing into a smooth paste. Add onion soup mix, cream of mushroom soup and cola-flavored carbonated beverage. Pour over the roast.

Step 4

Cover pan, and cook 1 hour in the preheated oven.

Step 5

Reduce oven temperature to 225 degrees F (110 degrees C), and continue cooking 2 hours. Remove from oven, and turn roast over so that the top is now covered with the gravy. Cover pan, and return to oven for a minimum of 2 hours.

Step 6

Remove from oven, and let meat rest for 10 minutes before slicing.

Nutrition Facts

Per Serving:

423.5 calories; protein 38.8g 78% DV; carbohydrates 12.7g 4% DV; fat 23.3g 36% DV; cholesterol 121.1mg 40% DV; sodium 735.8mg 29% DV.

Clay Pot Meatloaf and Potatoes

Prep: 15 mins **Cook:** 1 hr **Additional:** 15 mins **Total:** 1 hr 30 mins

Servings: 4

Yield: 4 servings

Ingredients

- 1 pound ground beef
- 2 slices white bread, torn into crumbs
- 1 egg
- 2 tablespoons milk
- 1 (1 ounce) package onion soup mix, divided

- 4 eaches Yukon Gold potatoes, peeled and cut into eighths
- ¼ cup ketchup
- 1 sweet onion, sliced
- 4 sprigs fresh rosemary

Directions

Step 1

Soak clay pot in a large bowl of water for about 15 minutes. Remove pot from water.

Step 2

Mix ground beef, bread crumbs, egg, milk, and 1/2 of the onion soup mix together in a large bowl. Form mixture into a loaf and place in the clay pot. Arrange potatoes around loaf and sprinkle remaining onion soup mix over potatoes. Scatter onions over potatoes and add rosemary sprigs. Place lid on the clay pot.

Step 3

Place clay pot in the cold oven. Heat oven to 350 degrees F (175 degrees C).

Step 4

Bake in the oven until meatloaf is no longer pink in the center, about 1 hour. An instant-read thermometer inserted into the center should read at least 160 degrees F (70 degrees C).

Nutrition Facts

Per Serving:

492.7 calories; protein 26.3g 53% DV; carbohydrates 55.8g 18% DV; fat 18.6g 29% DV; cholesterol 115.2mg 38% DV; sodium 952.7mg 38% DV.

Chicken Pot Pie

Prep: 10 mins **Cook:** 30 mins **Total:** 40 mins

Servings: 6

Yield: 1 - 9 inch pie

Ingredients

- 1 recipe pastry for a 9 inch double crust pie
- 1 carrot, chopped
- 1 head fresh broccoli, chopped

- 2 breast, bone removeds boneless chicken breast halves, cooked and chopped
- 1 (10.75 ounce) can condensed cream of chicken soup
- ⅔ cup milk
- 1 cup shredded Cheddar cheese
- ½ teaspoon salt

Directions

Step 1

Preheat oven to 425 degrees F (220 degrees C).

Step 2

Steam carrots and broccoli in a covered pot for 3 minutes, until slightly tender but still firm.

Step 3

In a large bowl, mix together carrots, broccoli, chicken, soup, milk, cheese, and salt. Spoon mixture into pastry-lined 9 inch pie pan and cover with top crust. Seal edges and cut steam vents in top.

Step 4

Bake in preheated oven for 30 minutes, until golden brown.

Nutrition Facts

Per Serving:

594.6 calories; protein 32.1g 64% DV; carbohydrates 36.8g 12% DV; fat 35.3g 54% DV; cholesterol 81mg 27% DV; sodium 1035.5mg 41% DV.

Italian Style Pot Roast

Prep: 10 mins **Cook:** 2 hrs 40 mins **Total:** 2 hrs 50 mins

Servings: 8

Yield: 6 to 8 ervings

Ingredients

- 3 ½ pounds boneless chuck roast
- 2 tablespoons vegetable oil
- 1 (14.5 ounce) can stewed tomatoes
- 1 ½ cups pizza sauce

- ½ cup grated Parmesan cheese
- 4 teaspoons Worcestershire sauce
- 2 cloves garlic, minced
- 2 teaspoons salt
- 2 teaspoons dried oregano
- ½ teaspoon ground black pepper
- ½ pound fresh mushrooms, sliced
- 3 tablespoons cornstarch
- 3 tablespoons water
- 1 (12 ounce) package egg noodles

Directions

Step 1

Heat a Dutch oven over medium-high heat, and brown meat on all sides in hot oil.

Step 2

In large bowl combine tomatoes, pizza sauce, cheese, Worcestershire sauce, garlic, salt, oregano, and pepper. Pour over meat. Cover and simmer over medium heat for 2 hours, turning meat each half hour.

Step 3

Remove meat from pan, and cool slightly. Skim fat from pan juices. Measure juices, and add enough water to make 6 cups liquid. Return liquid to Dutch oven. Blend cornstarch and 3 tablespoons cold water; stir into pan juices. Cook and stir till thickened and bubbly.

Step 4

Slice meat thinly against the grain. Return meat to pot, and add mushrooms. Simmer for 30 minutes longer.

Step 5

Cook pasta in a large pot of boiling water until done. Drain. To serve, place meat slices over hot noodles, and pour some sauce over. Pass remaining sauce.

Nutrition Facts

Per Serving:

742.3 calories; protein 44.8g 90% DV; carbohydrates 42.5g 14% DV; fat 42.9g 66% DV; cholesterol 181.7mg 61% DV; sodium 1208mg 48% DV.

Oyster Stew for One or Two

Prep: 10 mins **Cook:** 15 mins **Total:** 25 mins

Servings: 2

Yield: 2 servings

Ingredients

- 2 tablespoons butter
- 1 (6 inch) celery rib, finely chopped
- 1 small clove garlic, minced
- 1 tablespoon all-purpose flour
- 1 cup milk
- ¼ cup half-and-half cream
- ¼ teaspoon onion powder
- 1 pinch dried parsley
- ½ teaspoon salt
- 1 cup fresh shucked oysters, undrained
- 1 pinch ground black pepper, to taste

Directions

Step 1

Melt the butter in a heavy-bottomed skillet or wok over medium-high heat; cook and stir the celery and garlic in the butter until the celery is soft, 5 to 7 minutes. Add the flour and stir, scraping the bottom of pan until flour is lightly toasted. Slowly add the milk and half-and-half to the roux, stirring constantly. Stir the onion powder, parsley, and salt into the mixture. Reduce heat to medium-low; continue cooking and stirring until the mixture bubbles and thickens, 5 to 7 minutes.

Step 2

Add the oysters with the liquid from the container to the mixture; cook until the edges of the oysters curl, about 5 minutes more. Season with pepper just before serving.

I Made It Print

Nutrition Facts

Per Serving:

324.8 calories; protein 17.5g 35% DV; carbohydrates 17.8g 6% DV; fat 20.4g 31% DV; cholesterol 113.5mg 38% DV; sodium 871.2mg 35% DV.

Kae's Turkey Pot Pie

Prep: 30 mins **Cook:** 40 mins **Additional:** 10 mins **Total:** 1 hr 20 mins

Servings: 8

Yield: 1 pot pie

Ingredients

- 1 ½ cups all-purpose flour
- ½ teaspoon salt
- ½ cup vegetable shortening
- ¼ cup water, or as needed
- ¼ cup butter
- ¼ cup all-purpose flour
- 1 teaspoon salt
- ½ teaspoon ground black pepper
- 1 teaspoon rubbed sage
- 1 cup chicken broth
- 1 cup evaporated milk
- 4 cups cooked turkey, cut into bite-size pieces
- 2 (15 ounce) cans mixed vegetables (such as Veg-All), drained

Directions

Step 1

Preheat oven to 425 degrees F (220 degrees C). Whisk together 1 1/2 cups of flour and 1/2 teaspoon of salt in a bowl.

Step 2

With a fork or pastry cutter, cut the shortening into the flour mixture until it becomes crumbly, then stir in water, a tablespoon at a time, just until the dough holds together. Divide dough in half; roll out each half with a rolling pin on a floured surface to make an 11-inch circle. Fit one crust into a 10-inch pie dish; place the other crust on a baking sheet or piece of parchment paper, and set aside.

Step 3

Melt butter in a large pot over medium heat. Combine 1/4 cup flour, 1 teaspoon of salt, black pepper, and sage in a small bowl until thoroughly mixed; stir the flour mixture into the melted butter until the mixture forms a smooth paste. Allow the mixture to bubble for about 1 minute, then stir in the chicken broth and evaporated milk. Bring the mixture to a boil, and whisk until thick, about 2 minutes. Remove the sauce from the heat; stir in the cooked turkey meat and mixed vegetables. Spoon the filling into the prepared pie dish. Top the pie with the remaining crust, then pinch and fold together the edges of the crusts to seal. Cut an X into the center of the top crust with a sharp knife.

Step 4

Bake in the preheated oven until the crust is browned and the filling is bubbling, 35 to 40 minutes. Let stand 10 minutes before serving.

Cook's Note

If you decide to use fresh veggies, make sure that you steam the pre-cut potatoes and carrots. And then I use frozen peas and corn. Make sure you microwave them to thaw them out. You can add whatever veggies you like. If you have a large gathering, double the crust and filling and put into a large glass baking dish. It will still work. Just make sure you add a couple of Xs to vent the top. You will love it!

Nutrition Facts

Per Serving:

463.3 calories; protein 27.1g 54% DV; carbohydrates 31.7g 10% DV; fat 25g 38% DV; cholesterol 77.6mg 26% DV; sodium 795.3mg 32% DV.

Mini Chicken Pot Pies

Prep: 20 mins **Cook:** 15 mins **Additional:** 5 mins **Total:** 40 mins

Servings: 5

Yield: 10 mini pies

Ingredients

Vegetable cooking spray

- 1 ½ cups cubed cooked chicken
- 1 (10.75 ounce) can Campbell's Condensed Cream of Chicken Soup (Regular or 98% Fat Free)
- ½ (16 ounce) package frozen mixed vegetables, thawed
- All-purpose flour
- 1 (12 ounce) package refrigerated biscuits
- ½ cup shredded Cheddar cheese

Directions

Step 1

Heat the oven to 350 degrees F. Spray 10 (2 1/2-inch) muffin-pan cups with the cooking spray. Stir the chicken, soup and vegetables in a medium bowl.

Step 2

Sprinkle the flour on the work surface. Roll or pat the biscuits to flatten slightly. Press the biscuits into the bottoms and up the sides of the muffin-pan cups. Spoon about 1/3 cup chicken mixture into each biscuit cup. Lightly press the chicken mixture down so it's level. Top each with about 2 teaspoons cheese.

Step 3

Bake for 15 minutes or until the biscuits are golden brown and the cheese is melted. Let the pot pies cool in the pan on a wire rack for 5 minutes.

Nutrition Facts

Per Serving:

402.2 calories; protein 18g 36% DV; carbohydrates 40.3g 13% DV; fat 19.2g 30% DV; cholesterol 38.6mg 13% DV; sodium 1208.7mg 48% DV.

Pot Roast in Foil

Prep: 10 mins **Cook:** 4 hrs **Total:** 4 hrs 10 mins

Servings: 8

Yield: 8 servings

Ingredients

- 3 pounds bottom round
- 1 (10.75 ounce) can condensed cream of mushroom soup
- 1 packet dry onion soup mix
- 2 tablespoons water

Directions

Step 1

Preheat oven to 300 degrees F (150 degrees C).

Step 2

Place a piece of foil, about 30 inches long, into the bottom of a 9x13 inch roasting pan. Place the roast on the foil in the pan.

Step 3

In a separate small bowl, combine the mushroom soup with the onion soup mix. Mix well and pour over the roast. Sprinkle with the water. Fold foil over and seal all edges.

Step 4

Bake at 300 degrees F (150 degrees C) for 4 hours.

Nutrition Facts

Per Serving:

388.8 calories; protein 35.1g 70% DV; carbohydrates 3.1g 1% DV; fat 25.1g 39% DV; cholesterol 108.9mg 36% DV; sodium 410.8mg 16% DV.

Pot Roast with Vegetables

Prep: 20 mins **Cook:** 5 hrs 35 mins **Additional:** 10 mins **Total:** 6 hrs 5 mins

Servings: 6

Yield: 6 servings

Ingredients

- 1 tablespoon vegetable oil
- 1 (3 1/2) pound boneless beef chuck roast
- salt and ground black pepper to taste
- 1 large onion, finely chopped
- 1 clove garlic, chopped, or to taste
- 2 ½ cups beef stock
- 1 (16 ounce) can diced tomatoes
- ¼ cup red wine vinegar
- 1 tablespoon brown sugar
- 2 eaches bay leaves
- ¾ pound carrots, cut diagonally into 1-inch-thick slices
- 1 pound small red potatoes, quartered lengthwise
- 1 (6 ounce) jar mushrooms, or more to taste
- 1 ½ tablespoons cornstarch
- 1 ½ tablespoons cold water
- 1 pinch celery salt, or to taste
- 1 pinch dried basil, or to taste
- 1 pinch dried thyme, or to taste

Directions

Step 1

Preheat oven to 300 degrees F (150 degrees C).

Step 2

Heat vegetable oil in a large, heavy pot or cast-iron Dutch oven over medium heat. Brown chuck roast in the hot oil completely, 5 to 8 minutes per side; season with salt and black pepper and transfer to a platter. Reserve oil in pot.

Step 3

Cook and stir onion and garlic in the oil until onions are golden, about 15 minutes. Stir beef stock, tomatoes, red wine vinegar, brown sugar, and bay leaves into onions and garlic; bring to a boil and place chuck roast into the mixture. Cover pot.

Step 4

Cook in the preheated oven until meat is very tender, 4 to 4 1/2 hours. Scatter carrot slices around the beef and bring to a boil over medium heat; return to oven for 30 more minutes. Distribute potatoes around the beef and vegetables, bring to a boil again over medium heat, and bake until potatoes are tender, about 30 more minutes.

Step 5

Transfer beef to a serving platter, cover loosely with a tent of aluminum foil, and set aside to rest for 10 minutes.

Step 6

Stir mushrooms into pan drippings; bring to a simmer over low heat. Whisk cornstarch into cold water in a small bowl and stir into the drippings. Season with celery salt, basil, and thyme. Simmer until thickened, about 5 minutes. Remove and discard bay leaves. Slice beef; serve on a platter surrounded by vegetables. Pour gravy over beef.

Nutrition Facts

Per Serving:

567.2 calories; protein 35.9g 72% DV; carbohydrates 30.3g 10% DV; fat 32.8g 51% DV; cholesterol 120.3mg 40% DV; sodium 450.7mg 18% DV.

One Oh One Cookies

Servings: 48

Yield: 8 dozen

Ingredients

- 1 cup white sugar
- 1 cup packed brown sugar
- 1 cup butter
- 1 cup vegetable oil
- 1 egg
- 1 teaspoon cream of tartar
- 3 teaspoons vanilla extract
- 1 cup flaked coconut
- 1 cup chopped walnuts
- 1 cup crisp rice cereal
- 1 cup rolled oats
- 3 ½ cups all-purpose flour
- 1 teaspoon salt
- 1 teaspoon baking soda

Directions

Step 1

Preheat oven to 350 degrees F. In a large bowl, mix all **ingredients** until well blended.

Step 2

Drop on greased cookie sheets and bake for 12 to 15 minutes.

Nutrition Facts

Per Serving:

175.1 calories; protein 1.8g 4% DV; carbohydrates 18.5g 6% DV; fat 10.8g 17% DV; cholesterol 14mg 5% DV; sodium 113.9mg 5% DV.

Denise Salad Number One

Prep: 10 mins **Total:** 10 mins

Servings: 6

Yield: 6 servings

Ingredients

- 2 bunches arugula - rinsed, dried and torn
- 2 (11 ounce) cans mandarin orange segments, drained
- 1 large red onion, thinly sliced
- 1 pint cherry tomatoes
- 2 medium (blank)s yellow bell peppers, seeded and diced
- 1 cup unsalted sunflower seeds
- ¼ pound crumbled goat cheese
- 2 avocado, NS as to Florida or Californias avocados - peeled, pitted and sliced

Directions

Step 1

In a large bowl, combine arugula, oranges, onion, tomatoes and yellow peppers. Toss with dressing of your choice. Top with sunflower seeds, goat cheese and avocados.

Nutrition Facts

Per Serving:

266 calories; protein 9.3g 19% DV; carbohydrates 26.2g 9% DV; fat 16.3g 25% DV; cholesterol 14.9mg 5% DV; sodium 136mg 5% DV.

One Cup Salad

Prep: 5 mins **Total:** 5 mins

Servings: 6

Yield: 6 cups

Ingredients

- 1 cup pineapple chunks, drained
- 1 cup Mandarin orange segments, drained
- 1 cup miniature marshmallows
- 1 cup sour cream
- 1 cup cornflakes cereal
- 1 cup flaked coconut

Directions

Step 1

Combine the pineapple, Mandarin oranges, marshmallows, and sour cream in a bowl. Gently fold the cornflakes cereal into the mixture. Sprinkle the coconut over the top; stir into the salad just before serving.

Nutrition Facts

Per Serving:

225.1 calories; protein 2.3g 5% DV; carbohydrates 29.4g 10% DV; fat 11.6g 18% DV; cholesterol 16.9mg 6% DV; sodium 102.1mg 4% DV.

Easy One-Pan Taco Skillet

Prep: 15 mins **Cook:** 15 mins **Total:** 30 mins

Servings: 6

Yield: 6 servings

Ingredients

- 1 pound extra lean ground beef
- 1 (8.8 ounce) pouch UNCLE BEN'S Ready Rice Long Grain & Wild
- ¾ cup water
- 1 (1.25 ounce) package taco seasoning mix
- ½ cup frozen whole kernel corn, thawed
- 1 cup shredded white Cheddar cheese
- 2 medium (4-1/8" long)s green onions, sliced
- 1 (12 ounce) bag tortilla chips

Directions

Step 1

Heat a large nonstick skillet over medium heat. Cook ground beef, crumbling as it cooks, until browned, about 8 minutes. Drain liquid from pan. Add water and taco seasoning to beef.

Step 2

Cook rice according to package **directions**. Add cooked rice to beef mixture; stir in corn. Increase heat and bring to a boil. Simmer until liquid is absorbed, about 7 minutes, stirring constantly. Remove pan from heat.

Step 3

Sprinkle in the cheese and mix to incorporate. Top with green onions if desired. Serve with tortilla chips.

Cook's Note:

You can use ground turkey instead of ground beef in this recipe.

Nutrition Facts

Per Serving:

675.6 calories; protein 29.8g 60% DV; carbohydrates 75.3g 24% DV; fat 28.3g 44% DV; cholesterol 75.6mg 25% DV; sodium 1296.4mg 52% DV.

Apple Flavored Pot Roast

Prep: 15 mins **Cook:** 4 hrs **Total:** 4 hrs 15 mins

Servings: 6

Yield: 6 servings

Ingredients

- 1 (3 pound) boneless beef chuck roast
- 1 (12 fluid ounce) can frozen apple juice concentrate, thawed
- 1 dash soy sauce
- 3 cloves garlic, chopped
- 1 (1 ounce) envelope dry onion soup mix
- 3 medium (2-1/4" to 3" dia, raw)s baking potatoes, peeled and diced
- 2 medium (blank)s carrots, peeled and sliced

Directions

Step 1

Preheat the oven to 325 degrees F (165 degrees C).

Step 2

Place the roast in a roasting pan or large casserole dish. Fill the dish with about 1/2 inch of water, then stir in the apple juice concentrate. Sprinkle soy sauce over the top of the roast. Make several small slits in the roast and stuff pieces of garlic into them. Season the roast with onion soup mix. Cover with aluminum foil or a lid.

Step 3

Bake for 2 hours in the preheated oven, then remove from the oven and add the carrots and potatoes. Cover again, and continue to cook for an additional 2 hours, or until roast is fork tender.

Nutrition Facts

Per Serving:

792.1 calories; protein 41.8g 84% DV; carbohydrates 51.1g 17% DV; fat 46.2g 71% DV; cholesterol 163.6mg 55% DV; sodium 611.2mg 24% DV.

Oven Bag Pot Roast

Prep: 15 mins **Cook:** 2 hrs 30 mins **Total:** 2 hrs 45 mins

Servings: 8

Yield: 8 servings

Ingredients

- ½ cup all-purpose flour
- ground black pepper to taste
- 1 pinch paprika, or to taste
- 1 pinch garlic powder, or to taste
- 1 pinch onion powder, or to taste
- 3 pounds chuck roast
- ¼ cup butter
- 1 (10.75 ounce) can condensed beef consomme
- 1 cup water
- 1 ½ (1 ounce) envelopes dry onion soup mix
- 5 cloves garlic, peeled
- 1 teaspoon Worcestershire sauce
- 2 medium (blank)s carrots, chopped, or to taste
- ¼ onion, chopped, or to taste
- 3 medium (blank)s mushrooms, sliced, or to taste

Directions

Step 1

Preheat oven to 325 degrees F (165 degrees C).

Step 2

Whisk flour, black pepper, paprika, garlic powder, and onion powder together in a bowl. Dredge roast through the flour mixture to evenly coat.

Step 3

Melt butter in a large pot over medium-high heat; brown roast in the melted butter, about 5 minutes per side. Transfer roast to an oven bag and put into a 13x9-inch casserole dish.

Step 4

Whisk beef consomme, water, onion soup mix, garlic, and Worcestershire sauce together in a bowl; pour into the oven bag over the roast. Cut 6 small slits in the top of the oven bag for ventilation.

Step 5

Bake roast in the preheated oven for 1 hour 45 minutes; add carrots, onion, and mushrooms to the oven bag and bake until vegetables are tender and roast is cooked through, about 45 minutes. An instant-read thermometer inserted into the center should read 145 degrees F (63 degrees C).

Cook's Notes:

You may also add potatoes or any other other vegetable to the bag. You can also add to the water to reduce saltiness to your liking.

Nutrition Facts

Per Serving:

354.3 calories; protein 26.6g 53% DV; carbohydrates 13.2g 4% DV; fat 21.3g 33% DV; cholesterol 94.1mg 31% DV; sodium 772.8mg 31% DV.

Pot Roast Caribe

Prep: 25 mins **Cook:** 8 hrs **Total:** 8 hrs 25 mins

Servings: 6

Yield: 6 servings

Ingredients

- 2 tablespoons vegetable oil
- 1 (3 pound) boneless beef chuck roast
- 2 cloves garlic, crushed
- 1 cup chopped onion
- 1 teaspoon salt
- 2 (8 ounce) cans tomato sauce
- 2 tablespoons white sugar
- 1 tablespoon all-purpose flour
- 1 teaspoon unsweetened cocoa powder
- 1 teaspoon chili powder
- 1 teaspoon dried oregano
- 1 teaspoon ground cumin
- 1 teaspoon ground coriander
- ¼ teaspoon ground cinnamon
- 1 teaspoon grated orange zest
- 2 large potatoes, cut into large chunks

- 3 carrot, (7-1/2")s carrots, sliced
- 1 stalk celery, chopped
- ½ cup sliced almonds

Directions

Step 1

Heat the oil in a large skillet over medium-high heat. Place the roast into the hot oil and cook, turning frequently, until browned on all sides. Remove from the skillet and place in a slow cooker.

Step 2

Cook garlic and onions in the skillet in the meat drippings until tender. Stir in the salt and tomato sauce. Combine the sugar, flour, cocoa powder, chili powder, oregano, cumin, coriander, cinnamon, and orange zest; stir into the tomato sauce. Pour the tomato sauce over the roast in the slow cooker. Add potatoes, carrots and celery. Cover, and cook on Low for 6 to 8 hours, or until meat is tender. Garnish with sliced almonds before serving.

Nutrition Facts

Per Serving:

594.6 calories; protein 32.9g 66% DV; carbohydrates 39.8g 13% DV; fat 34.2g 53% DV; cholesterol 103.4mg 35% DV; sodium 887.6mg 36% DV.

Cola Pot Roast

Prep: 30 mins **Cook:** 2 hrs 30 mins **Total:** 3 hrs **Servings:** 8

Yield: 8 servings

Ingredients

- 1 (14.5 ounce) can stewed tomatoes
- 1 cup cola-flavored carbonated beverage
- 1 packet dry spaghetti sauce mix
- 1 cup chopped onion
- ¾ cup chopped celery
- 1 ½ teaspoons salt
- ½ teaspoon garlic salt
- 3 pounds beef chuck roast
- 2 tablespoons vegetable oil

Directions

Step 1

In a large bowl, break up tomatoes in their juice. Stir in cola, spaghetti sauce mix, onion, celery, salt, and garlic salt. Stir until spaghetti sauce mix is dissolved.

Step 2

In a Dutch oven, over medium high heat, brown meat in oil about 10 minutes on each side. Drain off all fat. Pour tomato mixture over meat. Cover, and reduce heat to low. Simmer slowly for about 2 1/2 hours, or until meat is tender.

Nutrition Facts

Per Serving:

324.2 calories; protein 21.1g 42% DV; carbohydrates 12.2g 4% DV; fat 21g 32% DV; cholesterol 77.3mg 26% DV; sodium 1166.1mg 47% DV.

Mother's Pot Roast

Prep: 10 mins **Cook:** 7 hrs **Total:** 7 hrs 10 mins

Servings: 5

Yield: 4 to 6 servings

Ingredients

- 2 ½ pounds tip round roast
- salt and pepper to taste
- 1 (15 ounce) can tomato sauce
- 1 onion, cut into thin strips
- 2 leaf (blank)s bay leaves
- 3 tablespoons all-purpose flour

Directions

Step 1

Spray slow cooker with non-stick cooking spray. Season roast with salt and pepper. Place meat in pot with fat side up. Pour tomato sauce over roast. Place onion rings over all. Toss in bay leaves. Cover and cook 1 hour on high.

Step 2

After 1 hour, reduce heat to low and cook 6 to 8 more hours. Carefully lift meat out of pot and remove to a warm platter.

Step 3

Pour drippings through strainer into medium-sized saucepan and discard material in strainer. Whisk in flour to liquid. Cook, stirring constantly over medium heat until thickened. Season to taste with salt and pepper; serve alongside roast.

Nutrition Facts

Per Serving:

552 calories; protein 45.2g 91% DV; carbohydrates 10.2g 3% DV; fat 36.6g 56% DV; cholesterol 149.7mg 50% DV; sodium 570.4mg 23% DV.

Chicken Pot Pie Casserole

Prep: 15 mins **Cook:** 45 mins **Total:** 1 hr

Servings: 6

Yield: 6 servings

Ingredients

- 2 large eggs eggs
- 3 cups frozen shredded hash browns
- salt and ground black pepper to taste
- 1 (16 ounce) package frozen mixed vegetables
- 1 (10.75 ounce) can cream of mushroom soup
- 1 cup chopped cooked chicken
- ½ cup bread crumbs
- 2 tablespoons butter, melted

Directions

Step 1

Preheat oven to 400 degrees F (200 degrees C). Grease a 9-inch square baking dish.

Step 2

Beat eggs together in a bowl. Add hash browns and mix well; season with salt and pepper. Press hash brown mixture into the prepared baking dish.

Step 3

Bake in the preheated oven until crust is lightly browned, about 15 minutes.

Step 4

Mix vegetables, cream of mushroom soup, and chicken together in a bowl and spread over the crust; top with bread crumbs. Drizzle butter over bread crumb layer and season with salt and pepper.

Step 5

Bake in the preheated oven until heated through and bread crumbs are lightly browned, about 30 minutes.

Nutrition Facts

Per Serving:

290.4 calories; protein 14.6g 29% DV; carbohydrates 34g 11% DV; fat 15.9g 25% DV; cholesterol 89.7mg 30% DV; sodium 519.1mg 21% DV.

Campfire Chicken Pot Pie

Prep: 10 mins **Cook:** 45 mins **Total:** 55 mins

Servings: 6

Yield: 6 servings

Ingredients

- 2 (29 ounce) cans mixed vegetables (with potatoes)
- 1 (10.75 ounce) can cream of chicken soup
- 1 (10.75 ounce) can cream of mushroom soup
- 2 large cooked chicken breasts, cut into cubes
- 1 (10 ounce) can refrigerated biscuit dough

Directions

Step 1

Stir vegetables, chicken soup, mushroom soup, and chicken cubes together in a Dutch oven with a flat lid.

Step 2

Cook over campfire coals until warmed through but not boiling, about 15 minutes.

Step 3

Arrange biscuit dough segments in a layer atop the vegetable mixture. Put lid on the Dutch oven and carefully arrange some hot coals atop the lid.

Step 4

Heat until the biscuits are cooked through, 15 to 30 minutes.

Nutrition Facts

Per Serving:

473 calories; protein 29.1g 58% DV; carbohydrates 46.8g 15% DV; fat 18.4g 28% DV; cholesterol 59.5mg 20% DV; sodium 1787.5mg 72% DV.

Fast and Easy Turkey Pot Pie

Prep: 15 mins **Cook:** 40 mins **Total:** 55 mins

Servings: 6

Yield: 1 8-inch pot pie

Ingredients

- 1 (15 ounce) package pastry for a 9 inch double crust pie
- 2 cups cooked turkey, cut into bite-size pieces
- 1 (10.75 ounce) can condensed cream of chicken soup
- 1 teaspoon seasoned salt
- 1 teaspoon seasoned pepper blend
- ½ cup shredded Cheddar cheese
- 1 (16 ounce) package frozen mixed vegetables, thawed and drained

Directions

Step 1

Preheat oven to 350 degrees F (175 degrees C). Line an 8-inch pie dish with 1 pastry crust; set the other crust aside.

Step 2

In a bowl, mix together the turkey, cream of chicken soup, seasoned salt and pepper, Cheddar cheese, and mixed vegetables. Pour the mixture into the prepared pie dish. Top the pie with the remaining pie crust, then pinch and fold the edges of the crusts together to seal. Cut a slit into the top of the pie crust with a sharp knife to vent the steam.

Step 3

Bake in the preheated oven until the crust is golden brown and the filling is bubbling, about 40 minutes.

Nutrition Facts

Per Serving:

540.5 calories; protein 23.8g 48% DV; carbohydrates 44.4g 14% DV; fat 30.3g 47% DV; cholesterol 49.4mg 17% DV; sodium 950mg 38% DV.

One-Dish Beef Stroganoff and Noodles

Prep: 10 mins **Cook:** 25 mins **Total:** 35 mins

Servings: 4

Yield: 4 servings

Ingredients

- ¾ pound boneless beef top round steak, 3/4 inches thick
- 1 (10.75 ounce) can Campbell's Healthy Request Condensed Cream of Mushroom Soup
- Chopped fresh parsley
- 1 (14 ounce) can Swanson Beef Broth
- ½ cup water
- 1 medium onion, sliced
- 3 cups uncooked medium egg noodles
- ½ cup plain yogurt

Directions

Step 1

Slice beef into very thin strips.

Step 2

Cook beef in nonstick skillet until browned, stirring often. Remove beef.

Step 3

Add soup, broth, water and onion. Heat to a boil. Stir in noodles. Cook over low heat 10 minutes or until noodles are done, stirring often. Stir in yogurt. Return beef to skillet and heat through. Garnish with parsley.

Nutrition Facts

Per Serving:

358.4 calories; protein 37.7g 76% DV; carbohydrates 29.7g 10% DV; fat 8.6g 13% DV; cholesterol 102.1mg 34% DV; sodium 747.3mg 30% DV.

Simple, Classic Chicken Potpie

Prep: 45 mins **Cook:** 38 mins **Total:** 1 hr 23 mins

Servings: 12

Yield: 2 pies

Ingredients

- 6 cups roasted, shredded rotisserie chicken
- 1 (15 ounce) package refrigerated pie crusts
- 2 tablespoons vegetable oil
- 2 medium onions, chopped
- 3 small stalks celery, cut crosswise 1/4-inch thick
- 2 cups chicken broth
- 1 (12 fluid ounce) can evaporated milk
- ⅓ cup butter
- 9 tablespoons all-purpose flour
- ¾ teaspoon dried thyme
- ¼ cup dry sherry or white wine
- Salt and ground pepper
- ¼ cup chopped fresh parsley
- 1 (16 ounce) package frozen peas and carrots, not thawed

Directions

Step 1

Adjust oven rack to low-center position; heat oven to 400 degrees. If using whole rotisserie chickens, separate meat from skin and bones, and tear into bite-size pieces. Discard skin and bones. Then remove pie dough from its box and follow **directions** for bringing to room temperature.

Step 2

Heat oil in Dutch oven over medium-high heat. Add onions and celery; saute until just tender, about 5 minutes. Transfer to a large bowl along with the chicken; set aside.

Step 3

Meanwhile, microwave chicken broth and milk in a microwave-safe bowl until steamy, 3 to 4 minutes. Heat butter over medium heat in the empty pan. When foaming subsides, whisk in flour and thyme; cook until golden, about 1 minute. Whisk in hot milk mixture. Bring to simmer, then continue to simmer until sauce fully thickens, about1 minute. Turn off heat, stir in sherry or wine, and season to taste with salt and pepper.

Step 4

Stir chicken mixture, parsley and the peas and carrots into the sauce. Divide mixture between two 9-inch deep-dish pie plates. Top each with pie dough, and flute crust by pinching with your fingers. Set on a baking sheet and bake until pastry is golden brown and filling is bubbly, 30 to 35 minutes. (Optional: Wrap second potpie in freezer wrap and freeze for a later meal. Remove wrapping, place potpie on a baking sheet and bake at 400 degrees until golden and bubbly, about 1 hour.)

Nutrition Facts

Per Serving:

479.5 calories; protein 23.6g 47% DV; carbohydrates 29.4g 10% DV; fat 29.6g 46% DV; cholesterol 77.3mg 26% DV; sodium 398.2mg 16% DV.

Best Braised Balsamic Pot Roast

Prep: 15 mins **Cook:** 3 hrs 50 mins **Total:** 4 hrs 5 mins

Servings: 6

Yield: 6 servings

Ingredients

- 3 tablespoons olive oil
- 1 (3 1/2) pound beef chuck roast
- salt and ground black pepper to taste
- 1 cup all-purpose flour
- 1 large onion, sliced
- 2 tablespoons red wine vinegar
- 2 tablespoons balsamic vinegar
- 1 (28 ounce) can crushed tomatoes
- 2 teaspoons dried thyme leaves
- 2 teaspoons hot pepper sauce, or to taste

Directions

Step 1

Preheat oven to 350 degrees F (175 degrees C).

Step 2

Heat olive oil in large, heavy pot over medium-high heat. Season roast with salt and black pepper. Place flour into a shallow bowl and press roast into the flour to coat completely. Cook the meat in the hot oil until browned completely, about 5 minutes per side.

Step 3

Spread onion slices over the roast; pour red wine vinegar into the pot around the roast. Drizzle half the balsamic vinegar over the roast and pour the remainder around it. Spread half the crushed tomatoes over the roast and distribute the remaining tomatoes around it. Sprinkle thyme leaves over roast; drizzle hot sauce atop thyme.

Step 4

Cover the pot and roast in the preheated oven until the meat is very tender, about 3 1/2 hours.

Nutrition Facts

Per Serving:

592.5 calories; protein 35.4g 71% DV; carbohydrates 29.2g 9% DV; fat 37.1g 57% DV; cholesterol 120.3mg 40% DV; sodium 290.7mg 12% DV.

Easy Pressure Cooker Pot Roast

Prep: 15 mins **Cook:** 1 hr 5 mins **Total:** 1 hr 20 mins

Servings: 8

Yield: 8 servings

Ingredients

- 2 tablespoons vegetable oil
- 1 (3 pound) boneless beef chuck roast, trimmed
- ground black pepper to taste
- 1 pinch seasoned salt, or to taste
- 1 pinch onion powder, or to taste
- 1 (14.5 ounce) can beef broth
- 1 ½ tablespoons Worcestershire sauce

- 1 large onion, cut into 4 wedges
- 4 carrot, (7-1/2")s carrots, peeled and cut into bite-size pieces
- 4 large potatoes, peeled and cut into bite-size pieces

Directions

Step 1

Heat oil in a pressure cooker over medium-high heat. Brown roast on all sides in the hot oil; season with pepper, seasoned salt, and onion powder.

Step 2

Pour in beef broth and Worcestershire sauce, add the quartered onion, and seal the lid. Bring the cooker up to full pressure. Reduce heat to low, maintaining full pressure, and cook for 30 minutes.

Step 3

Use the quick-release method to lower the pressure. Mix in carrots and potatoes, seal the lid again, and return the pressure cooker to the heat. Bring the cooker up to full pressure and cook for an additional 15 minutes. Use the quick-release method again and transfer the roast and vegetables to a serving dish.

Nutrition Facts

Per Serving:

450.2 calories; protein 25.1g 50% DV; carbohydrates 38.3g 12% DV; fat 21.8g 34% DV; cholesterol 77.5mg 26% DV; sodium 310.6mg 12% DV.

Healthier Chicken a la King

Prep: 5 mins **Cook:** 15 mins **Total:** 20 mins

Servings: 2

Yield: 2 servings

Ingredients

- 3 tablespoons chopped onion
- 2 tablespoons all-purpose flour
- 1 teaspoon salt
- 1 cup milk
- ½ pound cooked, cubed chicken meat
- 1 hard-boiled egg, sliced

- 1 ⅓ cups cooked spinach
- 3 tablespoons chopped onions

Directions

Step 1

Place onion in a medium saucepan over low heat and sprinkle with flour and salt. Stir together and add milk. Bring to a boil and cook until thickened.

Step 2

Mix in chicken, egg and spinach. Heat through and serve.

Nutrition Facts

Per Serving:

355.1 calories; protein 47.1g 94% DV; carbohydrates 19.3g 6% DV; fat 9.5g 15% DV; cholesterol 212.2mg 71% DV; sodium 1413.1mg 57% DV.

Easy Vegetable Pot Pie

Prep: 5 mins **Cook:** 40 mins **Total:** 45 mins

Servings: 6

Yield: 6 servings

Ingredients

- 1 (10.75 ounce) can condensed cream of potato soup
- 1 (15 ounce) can mixed vegetables, drained
- ½ cup milk
- ½ teaspoon dried thyme
- ½ teaspoon ground black pepper
- 2 (9 inch) frozen prepared pie crusts, thawed
- 1 egg, lightly beaten

Directions

Step 1

Preheat oven to 375 degrees F (190 degrees C).

Step 2

In a medium bowl, combine potato soup, mixed vegetables, milk, thyme, and black pepper.

Step 3

Spoon filling into bottom pie crust. Cover with top crust, and crimp edges to seal. Slit top crust, and brush with beaten egg if desired.

Step 4

Bake for 40 minutes. Remove from oven, and cool for 10 minutes before serving.

Nutrition Facts

Per Serving:

380.2 calories; protein 6.1g 12% DV; carbohydrates 40.8g 13% DV; fat 21.1g 33% DV; cholesterol 34.6mg 12% DV; sodium 873mg 35% DV.

Shearers' Mince and Potato Hot Pot

Prep: 35 mins **Cook:** 40 mins **Total:** 1 hr 15 mins

Servings: 6

Yield: 6 servings

Ingredients

- 5 medium potatoes, peeled and thinly sliced
- 1 tablespoon olive oil
- 1 pound ground beef
- 1 onion, chopped
- 1 tablespoon tomato sauce
- 1 tablespoon Worcestershire sauce
- salt and pepper to taste
- ¼ cup butter
- ¼ cup all-purpose flour
- 2 cups milk
- 1 cup shredded sharp Cheddar cheese
- 1 (6 ounce) can mushrooms, drained
- 2 tablespoons butter, diced

Directions

Step 1

Preheat oven to 350 degrees F (175 degrees C). Place potato slices in a medium bowl with enough water to cover.

Step 2

Heat oil in a medium saucepan over medium heat. Stir in ground beef, onion, tomato sauce, and Worcestershire sauce. Season with salt and pepper. Cook until beef is evenly browned and onions are tender.

Step 3

In a separate medium saucepan over medium heat, melt 1/4 cup butter, and thoroughly blend in flour. Gradually stir in milk. Cook and stir 5 minutes, or until thickened. Reduce heat, and blend Cheddar cheese into the mixture. Season with salt and pepper to taste.

Step 4

Line a medium baking dish with 1/2 the potato slices. Pour in the ground beef mixture, and top with mushrooms. Cover with the cheese sauce mixture. Top with remaining potatoes. Dot with 2 tablespoons butter.

Step 5

Bake 30 to 40 minutes in the preheated oven, until lightly browned.

Nutrition Facts

Per Serving:

645.6 calories; protein 25g 50% DV; carbohydrates 42.9g 14% DV; fat 42g 65% DV; cholesterol 121.1mg 40% DV; sodium 455.3mg 18% DV.

Pumpkin Pot De Creme

Prep: 15 mins **Cook:** 45 mins **Additional:** 8 hrs 45 mins **Total:** 9 hrs 45 mins

Servings: 6

Yield: 6 servings

Ingredients

- 2 cups whipping cream
- ¼ cup sugar
- 1 teaspoon cinnamon
- ¼ teaspoon ground ginger
- ¼ teaspoon ground nutmeg
- ¼ teaspoon ground cloves
- 1 cup pumpkin puree
- ½ vanilla bean, split and scraped
- 1 teaspoon dark rum
- 5 large egg yolks egg yolks
- 2 tablespoons white sugar
- ½ cup chopped toasted pecans

- ¼ cup maple syrup

Directions

Step 1

Preheat oven to 325 degrees F (165 degrees C).

Step 2

Combine the whipping cream, 1/4 cup sugar, cinnamon, ginger, nutmeg, cloves, pumpkin puree, and the vanilla bean pod and seeds in a saucepan over medium-low heat; bring to a simmer; stir in the rum. Remove from the heat cover and stand 15 minutes.

Step 3

Beat together the egg yolks and 2 tablespoons sugar. Stir in 2 tablespoons of the cream mixture. Pour the egg yolk mixture into the saucepan with the cream mixture to make a custard; stir; simmer 3 to 5 minutes.

Step 4

Arrange 6 ramekins in a shallow baking dish. Pour the custard evenly into the ramekins. Pour boiling water into the baking dish to half-way up the sides of the ramekins. Loosely cover the baking dish with aluminum foil.

Step 5

Bake in the preheated oven until the custard is nearly set with a dime-sized circle of jiggly liquid remaining in the center of each ramekin, 25 to 40 minutes. Allow to sit, loosely covered with aluminum foil, another 30 minutes.

Step 6

Cover each ramekin with plastic wrap; chill in refrigerator overnight. Top each custard with pecans and maple syrup to serve.

Nutrition Facts

Per Serving:

491.2 calories; protein 5.2g 10% DV; carbohydrates 30.3g 10% DV; fat 40.4g 62% DV; cholesterol 279.4mg 93% DV; sodium 136.7mg 6% DV.

Awesome Slow Cooker Pot Roast Plus Extras

Prep: 15 mins **Cook:** 3 hrs **Total:** 3 hrs 15 mins

Servings: 16

Yield: 16 servings

Ingredients

- 2 (10.75 ounce) cans condensed cream of mushroom soup
- 1 ¼ cups water
- 1 (1 ounce) package dry onion soup mix
- 5 ½ pounds pot roast
- 2 eaches potatoes, cut into cubes
- 2 carrot, (7-1/2")s carrots, sliced and halved
- 1 yellow squash, sliced
- 1 zucchini, halved lengthwise and sliced

Directions

Step 1

Stir cream of mushroom soup, water, and dry onion soup mix together in a slow cooker. Set pot roast into the soup mixture and spoon liquid over the meat. Add potatoes, carrots, yellow squash, and zucchini.

Step 2

Cook on High until the beef is cooked through, 3 to 4 hours. An instant-read thermometer inserted into the center should read 160 degrees F (70 degrees C). You can also cook on Low for 5 to 6 hours.

Nutrition Facts

Per Serving:

401.5 calories; protein 57.1g 114% DV; carbohydrates 9.9g 3% DV; fat 13.4g 21% DV; cholesterol 140.3mg 47% DV; sodium 480mg 19% DV.

Hamburger Pot Pie

Prep: 5 mins **Cook:** 40 mins **Additional:** 10 mins **Total:** 55 mins

Servings: 12

Yield: 2 - 9 inch pies

Ingredients

- 2 pounds lean ground beef
- 1 (1 ounce) package dry onion soup mix
- ½ cup milk
- salt and pepper to taste
- 2 (9 inch) unbaked 9 inch pie crusts
- 1 (2 pound) package frozen Southern-style hash brown potatoes

Directions

Step 1

Preheat an oven to 350 degrees F (175 degrees C).

Step 2

Mix beef, onion soup mix, milk, salt, and pepper together in a bowl. Evenly divide meat mixture into the pie crusts and top with hash browns.

Step 3

Bake in the preheated oven until no longer pink in the center, about 40 minutes. An instant-read thermometer inserted into the center should read at least 160 degrees F (70 degrees C). Allow pies to rest for 10 minutes before serving.

Nutrition Facts

Per Serving:

422.5 calories; protein 17.2g 34% DV; carbohydrates 28.9g 9% DV; fat 30.5g 47% DV; cholesterol 57.6mg 19% DV; sodium 442.1mg 18% DV.

Three-Pepper Rice and Chicken Pot

Prep: 45 mins **Cook:** 40 mins **Additional:** 5 mins **Total:** 1 hr 30 mins

Servings: 8

Yield: 8 servings

Ingredients

- ½ pound andouille sausage links
- 1 poblano chile
- 1 red bell pepper
- 3 tablespoons canola oil
- 1 ½ pounds skinless, boneless chicken thighs, cut into 1 1/2-inch chunks
- 3 tablespoons Cajun-style seasoning
- 1 ½ tablespoons butter
- 2 eaches yellow onions, finely chopped
- 2 medium (4-1/2" long)s banana (or hot) peppers, seeded and chopped
- 2 rib (blank)s celery ribs, finely chopped
- 6 cloves garlic, minced
- 1 shallot, minced
- 3 cups long grain white rice
- 1 ½ tablespoons butter
- 3 cups chicken stock
- 1 (10 ounce) can tomato sauce
- 1 (10 ounce) can diced tomatoes with mild green chilies, undrained
- 1 (12 fluid ounce) can or bottle beer
- salt to taste
- 1 cup frozen corn kernels, thawed

Directions

Step 1

Preheat your oven's broiler. Line a baking sheet with a sheet of foil.

Step 2

Cook andouille sausage in a skillet over medium heat until cooked through, about 15 minutes. Remove from skillet and cut into 1/4-inch slices; set aside.

Step 3

While the sausage is cooking, cut the peppers in half lengthwise and remove the stem and seeds. Place peppers, cut-side-down onto baking sheet and place into preheated oven. Broil peppers until the skins blacken, about 7 minutes, then place into a bowl and cover with plastic wrap. Allow the peppers to steam for 10 minutes until the skins loosen, then remove and discard blackened skins; chop peppers into 1/2 inch pieces and set aside.

Step 4

Heat the canola oil in a stockpot over high heat. Toss the chicken with Cajun seasoning and sear in batches in the oil until light brown and no longer pink in the center, about 6 minutes. Remove chicken, leaving oil in the stockpot, and drain on paper towels.

Step 5

Add 1 1/2 tablespoons of butter to the oil. Stir in the onion, banana peppers, celery, garlic, and shallot; cook until the onions are translucent, 3 to 4 minutes. Stir in rice and 1 1/2 tablespoon butter. Stir in the chicken stock, tomato sauce, and diced tomato with chilies. Cover and simmer until liquid is mostly absorbed into the rice, 10 to 12 minutes. Stir in the beer and cover; cook another 5 minutes until the rice is tender. Season with salt, then mix in the corn, poblano, bell pepper, chicken, and andouille sausage. Return to a simmer, then turn off heat and allow to rest 5 minutes before serving.

Nutrition Facts

Per Serving:

475.1 calories; protein 24.5g 49% DV; carbohydrates 38.5g 12% DV; fat 24.4g 38% DV; cholesterol 79.5mg 27% DV; sodium 1375.3mg 55% DV.

Impossibly Easy Chicken Pot Pie

Prep: 5 mins **Additional:** 30 mins **Total:** 35 mins

Servings: 6

Yield: 6 servings

Ingredients

- 1 ⅔ cups Green Giant™ Steamers™ frozen mixed vegetables
- 1 cup cut-up cooked chicken
- 1 (10.75 ounce) can condensed cream of chicken soup
- 1 cup Original Bisquick mix
- ½ cup milk
- 1 egg

Directions

Step 1

Heat oven to 400 degrees F. Mix vegetables, chicken and soup in ungreased glass pie plate, 9x1-1/4 inches.

Step 2

Stir together remaining **ingredients** with fork until blended. Pour into pie plate.

Step 3

Bake 30 minutes or until golden brown.

Tips

High Altitude (3500-6500 ft): Heat oven to 425 degrees F.

Nutrition Facts

Per Serving:

208.8 calories; protein 12.4g 25% DV; carbohydrates 22g 7% DV; fat 8g 12% DV; cholesterol 56.5mg 19% DV; sodium 622.1mg 25% DV.

2-Step Inside-Out Chicken Pot Pie

Cook: 20 mins **Total:** 20 mins

Servings: 4

Yield: 4 servings

Ingredients

- 1 pound skinless, boneless chicken breast, cut-up
- 1 (10.75 ounce) can Campbell's Condensed Cream of Chicken Soup (Regular or 98% Fat Free)
- 1 (16 ounce) package frozen vegetable combination (broccoli, cauliflower, carrots)
- 8 biscuit (2-1/2" dia)s hot biscuits, split

Directions

Step 1

Cook chicken in nonstick skillet until browned, stirring often.

Step 2

Add soup and vegetables. Cover and simmer until done. Serve on biscuits.

Nutrition Facts

Per Serving:

685.9 calories; protein 36g 72% DV; carbohydrates 74.9g 24% DV; fat 27.4g 42% DV; cholesterol 68.3mg 23% DV; sodium 1331.8mg 53% DV.

Marie-Eve's Turkey Pot Pie

Prep: 30 mins **Cook:** 1 hr 20 mins **Total:** 1 hr 50 mins

Servings: 8

Yield: 1 8-inch pie

Ingredients

- 1 teaspoon olive oil
- ½ cup chopped onion
- 1 clove garlic, minced, or to taste
- 1 ¼ cups water
- 1 (10.75 ounce) can condensed cream of mushroom soup
- 2 tablespoons chicken bouillon granules
- 2 eaches potatoes, peeled and cubed
- ½ cup chopped celery
- 1 cup peeled chopped carrot
- ½ cup frozen green peas, thawed
- 1 ½ cups cubed cooked turkey
- 2 cups all-purpose flour
- 1 tablespoon baking powder
- 1 teaspoon salt
- ¼ teaspoon dried basil
- ¼ teaspoon dried oregano
- ½ cup cold butter
- ¾ cup milk, or as needed
- 1 egg

Directions

Step 1

Heat olive oil in a large skillet over medium heat, and cook the onions and garlic until the onions are translucent, about 5 minutes. Pour in water, then whisk in the cream of mushroom soup and chicken granules until the mixture is smooth. Bring to a boil, then stir in potatoes, celery, carrot, and green peas; reduce heat, and simmer until thickened, 30 minutes to an hour. Stir in turkey, then simmer for another 30 minutes.

Step 2

Place an oven rack at the top position of the oven, and preheat oven to 400 degrees F (200 degrees C).

Step 3

Whisk the flour, baking powder, salt, basil, and oregano together in a bowl. Cut in the butter with a pastry cutter or fork until the mixture resembles coarse crumbs; mix in the milk and egg to make a soft dough. Turn the dough out onto a floured work surface, and knead until smooth, then roll out to a 9-inch round crust. Spoon the turkey filling into an 8-inch pie dish, and top the pie with the crust. Pinch the crust down at the edges around the pie dish, then cut several vents into the top of the pie.

Step 4

Bake in the preheated oven on the top rack until the filling is bubbling and the crust is golden brown, about 15 minutes.

Nutrition Facts

Per Serving:

383.9 calories; protein 15.4g 31% DV; carbohydrates 41.7g 14% DV; fat 17.4g 27% DV; cholesterol 75.7mg 25% DV; sodium 1151.8mg 46% DV.

"Black Friday" Turkey Pot Pie

Prep: 20 mins **Cook:** 40 mins **Additional:** 10 mins **Total:** 1 hr 10 mins

Servings: 12

Yield: 2 9-inch pies

Ingredients

- 1 tablespoon olive oil
- 1 ¾ cups diced onions
- 1 teaspoon minced garlic
- 1 (26 ounce) can cream of chicken soup
- ¼ cup white wine
- 2 teaspoons ground black pepper
- 1 teaspoon herbes de Provence
- 1 teaspoon poultry seasoning
- ½ teaspoon dried oregano
- ¼ teaspoon dried basil
- salt to taste
- 4 cups cubed cooked turkey
- 1 ¼ cups diced potatoes
- 1 cup frozen peas
- 1 cup diced carrots
- 2 double (blank)s pastries for 9-inch double-crust pies

Directions

Step 1

Preheat oven to 425 degrees F (220 degrees C).

Step 2

Heat olive oil in a deep skillet over medium heat; cook and stir onions and garlic until onions are translucent, about 5 minutes. Add cream of chicken soup, wine, black pepper, herbes de Provence, poultry seasoning, oregano, basil, and salt to onion mixture and bring to a simmer; remove skillet from heat.

Step 3

Gently stir turkey, potatoes, peas, and carrots into soup mixture until filling is evenly mixed.

Step 4

Fit 2 pie crusts into two 9-inch pie dishes. Pour filling into the pie crusts and top each with a second pie crust, pinching the edges together to seal. Cut several slits in the top crust of each pie for ventilation.

Step 5

Bake in the preheated oven until crusts are golden brown and filling is bubbling, 30 to 35 minutes. Cool pies for 10 minutes before serving.

Cook's Notes:

If the crust browns too quickly, cover it with aluminum foil.

Nutrition Facts

Per Serving:

490 calories; protein 20.3g 41% DV; carbohydrates 40.1g 13% DV; fat 27g 42% DV; cholesterol 40.4mg 14% DV; sodium 782.4mg 31% DV.

All-Natural Chicken Pot Pie

Prep: 30 mins **Cook:** 1 hr 20 mins **Additional:** 10 mins **Total:** 2 hrs

Servings: 8

Yield: 1 9-inch square casserole

Ingredients

- 3 cups all-purpose flour
- ½ teaspoon kosher salt
- ¼ teaspoon ground cinnamon
- ¼ teaspoon ground nutmeg
- ½ cup vegetable shortening (such as Crisco), frozen and cut into 1/2-inch cubes
- ½ cup butter, frozen and cut into 1/2-inch cubes
- 6 tablespoons ice-cold water, or more as needed
- 3 breast half, bone and skin removed (blank)s skinless, boneless chicken breast halves
- 2 medium (blank)s carrots, diced
- 1 cup chopped celery
- 3 eaches potatoes, peeled and cut into 1/4-inch cubes
- 2 cups frozen petite peas
- ½ large onion, diced, divided
- 1 cup water
- 1 tablespoon butter
- 4 cloves garlic, minced
- 2 tablespoons all-purpose flour
- 2 teaspoons chicken soup base
- ½ teaspoon salt
- ½ teaspoon ground black pepper
- ½ teaspoon chopped fresh sage
- ½ teaspoon chopped fresh thyme

Directions

Step 1

Preheat an oven to 365 degrees F (185 degrees C). Lightly oil a 9-inch square casserole dish.

Step 2

Sift the 3 cups flour, cinnamon, and nutmeg together into a large mixing bowl. Cut the vegetable shortening and cold butter into the flour mixture with a knife or pastry blender until the mixture resembles coarse crumbs with some chunks the size of peas. Add the ice water a tablespoon at a time, tossing with a fork, until the flour mixture is moistened. Work the dough as little as possible; this is the key to a super light and flaky crust. After half the water has been incorporated, watch closely, as mixture will come together suddenly. Once it begins to stick together, gather into a ball, divide into halves, and roll each ball out to 1/4-inch thickness, adding flour as necessary to prevent sticking. Press one of the dough portions into the prepared casserole dish, covering bottom and sides completely.

Step 3

Heat a skillet over medium heat. Sear the chicken breasts in the hot skillet until evenly browned on both sides; cut into small cubes and set aside in a large mixing bowl. Reduce the heat under the skillet to medium-low. Cook the carrots, celery, potatoes, peas, and about half the diced onion in the drippings from the chicken until the carrots soften; add to the bowl with the chicken.

Step 4

Increase the heat to medium. Add the water to the skillet and bring to a boil while scraping the browned bits of food off of the bottom of the pan with a wooden spoon; pour into a cup and set aside.

Step 5

Melt the butter in the skillet. Cook and stir the remaining onion and the garlic in the melted butter until the onions begin to brown, 5 to 8 minutes. Sprinkle the 2 tablespoons flour over the onion mixture and stir to evenly coat. Pour the reserved liquid over the onion mixture. Stir the chicken base, salt, pepper, sage, and thyme into the mixture. Cook and stir until the mixture has reduced into a thick gravy; pour over the chicken mixture in the mixing bowl. Allow the mixture to cool completely.

Step 6

Pour the mixture over the crust in the casserole dish. Top with the remaining portion of dough and pinch the edges together to seal the edges. Cut a few slits into the top to vent.

Step 7

Bake in the preheated oven until the crust is golden brown and the gravy bubbles through the slits, about 1 hour. Allow to cool slightly before serving, 10 to 15 minutes.

Nutrition Facts

Per Serving:

570 calories; protein 19.4g 39% DV; carbohydrates 60.3g 19% DV; fat 28.1g 43% DV; cholesterol 61.6mg 21% DV; sodium 648.2mg 26% DV.

Roasted Portobello, Red Pepper, and Arugula Salad for One

Prep: 15 mins **Cook:** 30 mins **Total:** 45 mins

Servings: 1

Yield: 1 salad

Ingredients

- 1 portobello mushroom, stem removed
- 1 tablespoon olive oil
- 1 teaspoon red wine vinegar
- 1 clove garlic, thinly sliced
- ¼ shallot, thinly sliced
- salt and pepper to taste
- ½ roasted red pepper, cut into strips
- 3 cups arugula leaves
- 1 ounce grated Romano cheese
- 1 tablespoon Greek salad dressing

Directions

Step 1

Preheat oven to 425 degrees F (220 degrees C). Line a baking sheet with a piece of aluminum foil.

Step 2

Brush the mushroom on both sides with olive oil and place gill-side up onto the baking sheet. Drizzle with any remaining olive oil, and the red wine vinegar. Sprinkle with sliced garlic and shallot; season to taste with salt and pepper. Top with the piece of roasted red pepper, and wrap the foil tightly around the mushroom.

Step 3

Bake in preheated oven until the mushroom is tender, about 30 minutes.

Step 4

Toss the arugula with Romano cheese and salad dressing. Place onto a plate and top with the hot mushroom and pepper. Dig in!

Nutrition Facts

Per Serving:

352.5 calories; protein 14.5g 29% DV; carbohydrates 15.2g 5% DV; fat 27.5g 42% DV; cholesterol 29.5mg 10% DV; sodium 644.2mg 26% DV.

Pot Roast, Vegetables, and Beer

Prep: 20 mins **Cook:** 2 hrs 50 mins **Total:** 3 hrs 10 mins

Servings: 6

Yield: 6 servings

Ingredients

- 2 tablespoons olive oil
- 1 (3 pound) beef pot roast
- 1 onion, chopped
- 5 cloves garlic, minced
- 1 pound carrots, cut into chunks
- 1 (8 ounce) package sliced fresh mushrooms
- 1 ½ pounds potatoes, peeled and cut into chunks
- 2 tablespoons all-purpose flour
- 2 cups beef stock
- 1 (12 fluid ounce) can or bottle dark beer
- 1 bay leaf
- 3 tablespoons chopped fresh thyme
- 1 teaspoon brown sugar
- 2 tablespoons whole-grain Dijon mustard
- 1 tablespoon tomato paste
- salt and ground black pepper to taste

Directions

Step 1

Preheat an oven to 350 degrees F (175 degrees C).

Step 2

Heat the olive oil in a Dutch oven. Brown the pot roast on all sides in the hot oil; remove from pan and set aside. Cook the onion and garlic in the hot oil until they begin to soften and turn brown, about 5 minutes. Add the carrots, mushrooms, and potatoes to the pot; cook and stir until they begin to color, 2 to 3 minutes. Mix the flour into the vegetables; stir continuously for 1 minute. Pour the beef stock and beer into the mixture and bring to a boil, stirring continuously. Add the Bay leaf, thyme, brown sugar, mustard, tomato paste, salt, and pepper. Place the pot roast atop the entire mixture. Cover pot with lid.

Step 3

Bake in the preheated oven until the meat and vegetables are completely tender, about 2 1/2 hours.

Nutrition Facts

Per Serving:

567.7 calories; protein 33.8g 68% DV; carbohydrates 38.7g 13% DV; fat 29g 45% DV; cholesterol 98.2mg 33% DV; sodium 300mg 12% DV.

Easy Chicken Pot Pie

Prep: 10 mins **Cook:** 30 mins **Total:** 40 mins

Servings: 6

Yield: 6 servings

Ingredients

- 2 (9 inch) deep dish frozen pie crusts, thawed
- 1 (15 ounce) can mixed vegetables, drained
- 2 cups cooked, diced chicken breast
- 1 (10.75 ounce) can condensed cream of chicken soup
- ½ cup milk

Directions

Step 1

Preheat oven to 350 degrees F (175 degrees C).

Step 2

In a bowl combine the mixed vegetables, chicken, cream of chicken soup and milk. Pour mixture into one of the pie crusts. Turn the other crust over and pop out of the tin onto the top of the filled pie. Seal the edges and poke holes in top crust.

Step 3

Bake at 350 degrees F (175 degrees C) for 30 minutes or until crust is golden brown.

 I Made It Print

Nutrition Facts

Per Serving:

463.4 calories; protein 19.1g 38% DV; carbohydrates 39.7g 13% DV; fat 24.8g 38% DV; cholesterol 41.6mg 14% DV; sodium 920mg 37% DV.

Mahi Mahi Pot Pie

Prep: 10 mins **Cook:** 1 hr **Additional:** 10 mins **Total:** 1 hr 20 mins

Servings: 6

Yield: 1 9-inch pie

Ingredients

- 1 tablespoon vegetable oil
- 1 ½ pounds mahi mahi fillets
- 1 teaspoon dried thyme
- salt and ground black pepper to taste
- 1 (10.75 ounce) can condensed cream of potato soup
- ½ cup milk
- 1 (15 ounce) can mixed vegetables (with potatoes), drained
- 2 (9 inch) deep dish pie crusts

Directions

Step 1

Preheat an oven to 375 degrees F (190 degrees C).

Step 2

Heat the vegetable oil in a large skillet over medium heat.

Step 3

Season the mahi mahi fillets with the thyme, salt, and black pepper; lay the seasoned fillets in the hot skillet. Cover the skillet and cook the fillets for 7 minutes, turn the fillets, and continue cooking the other side until the flesh flakes easily with a fork, 5 to 7 minutes.

Step 4

Remove the mahi mahi to a cutting board and cut into bite-size pieces, removing any visible bones as you notice them.

Step 5

Stir the cream of potato soup, milk, and mixed vegetables together in a saucepan over medium heat; season with salt and pepper. Allow the mixture to simmer, stirring occasionally, 5 minutes.

Step 6

Gently fold the mahi mahi pieces into the soup mixture.

Step 7

Line a 9-inch deep-dish pie plate with one of the prepared pie crusts.

Step 8

Pour the soup mixture with the mahi mahi into the pie crust.

Step 9

Lay the remaining pie crust atop the assembled pie. Seal the edges with wet fingertips.

Step 10

Bake in the preheated oven until the crust is a golden brown and the pie is heated through, 40 to 45 minutes. Allow to cool 10 to 15 minutes before serving.

I Made It Print

Nutrition Facts

Per Serving:

688.8 calories; protein 29g 58% DV; carbohydrates 72.6g 23% DV; fat 32.7g 50% DV; cholesterol 109.9mg 37% DV; sodium 1148.5mg 46% DV.

Speedy Chili Pot Pie

Prep: 10 mins **Cook:** 20 mins **Total:** 30 mins

Servings: 6

Yield: 6 servings

Ingredients

- 2 (15 ounce) cans turkey chili with beans, undrained
- 1 (8.5 ounce) package corn bread/muffin mix
- ⅓ cup milk
- 1 egg
- 2 tablespoons shredded Cheddar cheese, or as desired
- 1 tablespoon sour cream, or as desired

Directions

Step 1

Preheat oven to 400 degrees F (200 degrees C).

Step 2

Pour the turkey chili into a 9-inch pie dish. In a bowl, whisk together the corn bread mix, milk, and egg until slightly lumpy; spoon the corn bread batter on top of the chili.

Step 3

Bake in the preheated oven until the edges of the corn bread begin to brown and the center is set, 20 to 25 minutes. Sprinkle with Cheddar cheese and a dollop of sour cream.

Nutrition Facts

Per Serving:

306.4 calories; protein 16.3g 33% DV; carbohydrates 42.2g 14% DV; fat 8g 12% DV; cholesterol 57.2mg 19% DV; sodium 1371.8mg 55% DV.

Angela's Amazing Chicken Pot Pie

Prep: 15 mins **Cook:** 1 hr 25 mins **Total:** 1 hr 40 mins

Servings: 6

Yield: 6 servings

Ingredients

- 6 eaches bone-in chicken thighs with skin
- 3 cups water, or amount to cover
- 1 ¼ cups milk
- ½ cup butter
- 6 eaches potatoes, peeled and cubed
- 1 (10.5 ounce) can condensed cream of chicken soup
- 1 ¼ cups self-rising flour

Directions

Step 1

Place chicken thighs into a large saucepan, pour in water to cover, and bring to a boil over medium heat. Reduce heat to a simmer, skim off any foam that forms, and cook the chicken until tender, about 45 minutes. Set chicken aside to cool, and reserve 2 cups of the chicken broth from the pan. Remove bones and skin from cooled chicken thighs, and chop the chicken meat coarsely.

Step 2

Place the potatoes into a large pot and cover with salted water. Bring to a boil over high heat, then reduce heat to medium-low, cover, and simmer until tender, 15 to 20 minutes. Drain and allow to steam dry for a minute or two.

Step 3

Preheat oven to 350 degrees F (175 degrees C).

Step 4

Bring milk and butter to a boil in a saucepan over medium heat, stirring until butter has melted. Let the mixture cool completely.

Step 5

Place chicken meat into the bottom of a 9x13-inch baking dish. Arrange potato cubes over the chicken. Pour the reserved chicken broth into a bowl, and whisk in the cream of chicken soup; pour the soup mixture over the chicken and potatoes. Pour cooled milk mixture into a large mixing bowl, and gradually whisk in self-rising flour, about 1/2 cup at a time, until the batter is smooth. Scrape the batter over the **ingredients** in the baking dish.

Step 6

Bake in the preheated oven until the pot pie is bubbling and the crust is browned, about 40 minutes.

Cook's Notes

Make sure you use enough water to boil the chicken so you'll have two cups of broth for the recipe. Otherwise, you'll need a large can of chicken broth.

The crust will be lumpy if you do not allow the milk and butter mixture to cool completely after bringing it to a boil. So you'll want to go ahead and prepare this as soon as you have the chicken and potatoes boiling.

Nutrition Facts

Per Serving:

650.5 calories; protein 29g 58% DV; carbohydrates 62.5g 20% DV; fat 31.5g 48% DV; cholesterol 119.7mg 40% DV; sodium 866.5mg 35% DV.

Stovetop Yankee Pot Roast

Prep: 25 mins **Cook:** 3 hrs **Additional:** 10 mins **Total:** 3 hrs 35 mins

Servings: 10

Yield: 1 pot roast

Ingredients

- ¼ cup olive oil
- 1 (3 pound) beef round tip roast
- flour for dredging
- 3 medium onions, sliced
- 3 large carrots, peeled and cut into small chunks
- 3 large stalks celery, diced
- 4 cloves garlic, minced
- 3 berry (blank)s whole allspice berries
- salt and pepper to taste
- 1 cup dry red wine
- 2 (12 ounce) cans beef broth
- 2 tablespoons cornstarch dissolved in a small amount of water

Directions

Step 1

Heat the oil in a heavy, cast iron pot over medium heat. Dredge the roast in the flour, shake off the excess, and brown in the hot oil on all sides. Stir in the onions, carrots, celery, garlic, and allspice; cook till lightly browned. Pour in the red wine and bring to a simmer before pouring in the beef broth. Reduce heat to low, cover and cook until the beef is tender, about 2 to 3 hours.

Step 2

When the meat has finished cooking, remove to a cutting board, and allow to rest for 10 minutes. While beef is resting, thicken the cooking liquid with the cornstarch. Slice the beef and serve with the gravy.

Nutrition Facts

Per Serving:

387.7 calories; protein 28.1g 56% DV; carbohydrates 10.1g 3% DV; fat 23.6g 36% DV; cholesterol 88.4mg 30% DV; sodium 390.5mg 16% DV.

Cranberry Pot Roast

Prep: 20 mins **Cook:** 4 hrs 15 mins **Total:** 4 hrs 35 mins

Servings: 10

Yield: 10 servings

Ingredients

- 3 cups beef broth
- 1 cup water
- 2 (14.5 ounce) cans cranberry sauce
- 1 (4 pound) beef chuck roast
- salt and ground black pepper to taste
- 3 tablespoons all-purpose flour
- 2 tablespoons vegetable oil
- 1 large sweet onion, chopped

Directions

Step 1

Bring the beef broth and water to a boil in a saucepan over high heat. Stir in the cranberry sauce until dissolved. Pour the sauce into a slow cooker set to High.

Step 2

Meanwhile, season the beef roast with salt and pepper, then sprinkle evenly with the flour. Heat the vegetable oil in large skillet over medium heat. Cook the roast in the hot oil until brown on all sides, about 2 minutes per side. Transfer the roast to the slow cooker along with the chopped onion.

Step 3

Cook until the roast easily pulls apart with a fork, about 4 hours.

Nutrition Facts

Per Serving:

587.4 calories; protein 32.5g 65% DV; carbohydrates 33.8g 11% DV; fat 35.4g 55% DV; cholesterol 128.8mg 43% DV; sodium 378.3mg 15% DV.

Rustic Chicken Pot Pie

Prep: 25 mins **Cook:** 30 mins **Additional:** 15 mins **Total:** 1 hr 10 mins

Servings: 4

Yield: 4 servings

Ingredients

- 2 strip (blank)s strips bacon
- 4 tablespoons unsalted butter plus additional for greasing
- 2 medium carrots, chopped
- 2 stalks celery, chopped
- 1 medium onion, chopped
- 3 cloves garlic, finely chopped
- 3 sprigs fresh thyme, leaves only
- 1 teaspoon red pepper flakes
- 1 (3 1/2) pound roasted chicken, meat hand-torn into bite-size pieces
- 2 tablespoons all-purpose flour plus additional for dusting pastry
- 1 cup chicken stock
- 2 cups shredded white Cheddar cheese, divided
- 1 (17.5 ounce) package frozen puff pastry, thawed
- 1 egg, slightly beaten
- Salt and black pepper to taste
- Reynolds Wrap Aluminum Foil

Directions

Step 1

In a large skillet over medium heat, crisp the bacon until golden brown. Drain and crumble the bacon; set aside. Add butter to the pan with the bacon drippings. Add carrots, celery, onion, garlic, thyme and red pepper flakes, making sure to scrape up any bits left over from the bacon. Season with salt and pepper. Allow the vegetables to cook for 10-15 minutes, or until slightly tender but still firm.

Step 2

Add the chicken and the flour to the vegetables. Mix to combine. Add the chicken stock and bring the mixture to a boil to thicken. Once the filling has thickened and most of the liquid has evaporated, take the skillet off the heat. Stir in half of the cheese. Season with salt and pepper to taste.

Step 3

Lightly dust your work surface with flour. Roll out 1 sheet of the puff pastry until it is large enough to cover a 9-inch dish. Place the pastry in the greased 9-inch dish. Fill pastry with filling. Top with the remaining cheese and bacon. Roll out the remaining sheet of puff pastry. Gently score the pastry in a crisscross pattern with a paring knife and place the pastry on top of the filling. Fold over and tuck in any remaining pastry.

Step 4

Brush with the slightly beaten egg. Place in the refrigerator for 15-30 minutes. Place the chilled potpie on a rimmed baking sheet lined with Reynolds Wrap Aluminum Foil. Bake in a 400 degree F oven for 20-25 minutes or until golden and puffy. Serve immediately.

Nutrition Facts

Per Serving:

1618.5 calories; protein 87.7g 175% DV; carbohydrates 66.8g 22% DV; fat 110.1g 169% DV; cholesterol 380.3mg 127% DV; sodium 1204mg 48% DV.

Pheasant Pot Pie

Prep: 15 mins **Cook:** 1 hr 15 mins **Total:** 1 hr 30 mins

Servings: 8

Yield: 1 9-inch pie

Ingredients

- 2 cups chicken broth
- 1 pound pheasant, cut into bite-size pieces
- 1 cup chopped carrots
- ½ cup chopped celery
- 1 (15 ounce) can peas, drained
- ⅓ cup salted butter
- ½ yellow onion, chopped
- ⅓ cup all-purpose flour
- ⅔ cup milk
- 1 teaspoon salt
- 1 teaspoon dried rosemary
- ½ teaspoon ground black pepper
- ½ teaspoon dried sage
- ½ teaspoon ground celery seed
- 2 double (blank)s 9-inch refrigerated pie crusts
- 1 egg white, beaten

Directions

Step 1

Preheat oven to 400 degrees F (200 degrees C).

Step 2

Bring broth to a boil in a pot; add pheasant, carrots, and celery and boil until pheasant is cooked through, about 15 minutes. Add peas to broth and boil for 1 minute. Drain and reserve broth from pot.

Step 3

Melt butter in a separate pot over medium heat; cook and stir onion until translucent, about 5 minutes. Gradually stir flour into butter until smooth. Pour reserved broth and milk into flour mixture, stirring constantly. Add salt, rosemary, pepper, sage, and celery seed to broth mixture and simmer over medium-low heat until sauce is thickened, about 5 minutes.

Step 4

Lower oven temperature to 375 degrees F (190 degrees C).

Step 5

Press 1 pie crust into a pie plate and lightly brush with egg white.

Step 6

Bake crust in the oven until lightly browned, about 5 minutes.

Step 7

Spoon about 1/4 of the pheasant-vegetable mixture into the baked pie crust. Mix remaining pheasant-vegetable mixture into the sauce; pour into baked pie crust. Place second crust on top of the filling, pinching the edges together to form a seal. Cut your initials into the top crust for ventilation.

Step 8

Bake in the oven until top is golden brown, about 40 minutes.

Nutrition Facts

Per Serving:

698.7 calories; protein 22.3g 45% DV; carbohydrates 54.3g 18% DV; fat 43.5g 67% DV; cholesterol 62.3mg 21% DV; sodium 967.3mg 39% DV.

Kitchen Easy Chicken Pot Pie

Prep: 10 mins **Cook:** 30 mins **Total:** 40 mins

Servings: 4

Yield: 4 servings

Ingredients

- 1 (10.75 ounce) can Condensed Cream of Chicken Soup (regular, 98% Fat Free, or 25% Less Sodium)*
- 1 (10 ounce) package frozen mixed vegetables, thawed
- 1 cup cubed cooked chicken or turkey
- ½ cup milk
- 1 egg
- 1 cup all-purpose baking mix

Directions

Step 1

Preheat oven to 400 degrees F.

Step 2

Mix soup, vegetables and chicken in 9-inch pie plate.

Step 3

Mix milk, egg and baking mix. Pour over chicken mixture. Bake 30 minutes or until golden.

Nutrition Facts

Per Serving:

339.1 calories; protein 18.5g 37% DV; carbohydrates 35.7g 12% DV; fat 14.3g 22% DV; cholesterol 81.3mg 27% DV; sodium 997.5mg 42% DV.

One - Two - Three - Mexican Macaroni Salad

Prep: 10 mins **Cook:** 10 mins **Additional:** 1 hr **Total:** 1 hr 20 mins

Servings: 10

Yield: 10 servings

Ingredients

- 1 (16 ounce) package dry macaroni
- 1 ½ cups chunky salsa
- 1 cup mayonnaise
- ½ cup finely chopped green bell pepper
- 1 teaspoon garlic powder
- 1 teaspoon salt
- ground black pepper to taste
- 1 (6 ounce) can sliced black olives, drained

Directions

Step 1

Bring a large pot of lightly salted water to a boil. Add pasta and cook for 8 to 10 minutes or until al dente; rinse under cold running water, and drain.

Step 2

In a large bowl, combine the salsa, mayonnaise, green pepper, garlic powder, salt, black pepper, and olives; mix well. Pour pasta into mixture, and stir to coat thoroughly. Cover, and refrigerate at least one hour before serving.

Nutrition Facts

Per Serving:

367.6 calories; protein 7.6g 15% DV; carbohydrates 39.3g 13% DV; fat 20.4g 31% DV; cholesterol 8.4mg 3% DV; sodium 740.6mg 30% DV.

Slow Cooker Au Jus Pot Roast

Prep: 15 mins **Cook:** 8 hrs 20 mins **Total:** 8 hrs 35 mins

Servings: 8

Yield: 8 servings

Ingredients

- 1 (4 pound) boneless beef chuck roast
- 1 tablespoon Worcestershire sauce, or to taste
- 1 tablespoon Montreal-style steak seasoning
- 2 tablespoons olive oil
- 1 cube beef bouillon
- 1 cup hot strong black coffee
- 1 (8 ounce) can tomato sauce
- 1 teaspoon dried oregano, or to taste
- 2 teaspoons Worcestershire sauce, or to taste

Directions

Step 1

Rub chuck roast with 1 tablespoon Worcestershire sauce and sprinkle on all sides with steak seasoning.

Step 2

Heat olive oil in a large skillet over medium-high heat. Sear the roast in the hot oil until browned, about 5 minutes per side. Transfer roast to a slow cooker.

Step 3

Dissolve beef bouillon cube in the coffee and pour the mixture over the roast. Pour tomato sauce over meat and season with oregano; drizzle meat with 2 teaspoons Worcestershire sauce.

Step 4

Set cooker to Low and cook until meat is tender, 8 to 10 hours.

Nutrition Facts

Per Serving:

385.6 calories; protein 26.9g 54% DV; carbohydrates 2.8g 1% DV; fat 29g 45% DV; cholesterol 103.4mg 35% DV; sodium 697.8mg 28% DV.

Never Fail Applesauce Spice Cake

Servings: 18

Yield: 1 - 9 x 13 inch cake

Ingredients

- 2 ½ cups all-purpose flour
- 1 ¾ cups white sugar
- 1 ½ teaspoons baking soda
- ¼ teaspoon salt
- ½ teaspoon baking powder
- ¾ teaspoon ground cinnamon
- ½ teaspoon ground cloves
- ½ teaspoon ground allspice
- ½ cup butter
- ½ cup buttermilk
- 1 ½ cups applesauce
- 2 large eggs eggs
- ¾ cup chopped walnuts
- ¼ cup butter
- 1 cup chopped pecans
- 4 cups confectioners' sugar
- 1 (8 ounce) package cream cheese, softened
- 1 ½ teaspoons vanilla extract

Directions

Step 1

Sift flour, white sugar, soda, salt, baking powder, and spices into a large mixing bowl. Mix in 1/2 cup butter or margarine, buttermilk, and applesauce. Beat for 2 minutes with an electric mixer on medium speed. Beat in eggs. Fold in 3/4 cup chopped nuts. Pour batter into a greased and floured 9 x 13 inch pan.

Step 2

Bake at 350 degrees F (175 degrees C) for 50 minutes.

Step 3

Mix confectioners' sugar, cream cheese, and vanilla until smooth. Melt 1/4 cup butter over medium heat, and add 1 cup chopped pecans. Keep stirring until browned. Stir cooled pecans into cream cheese mixture. Frost the cooled cake.

Nutrition Facts

Per Serving:

448.2 calories; protein 5.1g 10% DV; carbohydrates 64g 21% DV; fat 20.4g 31% DV; cholesterol 55mg 18% DV; sodium 258.3mg 10% DV.

Slow Cooker Sweet-and-Sour Pot Roast

Prep: 20 mins **Cook:** 10 hrs 15 mins **Total:** 10 hrs 35 mins

Servings: 6

Yield: 6 servings

Ingredients

- 6 small white potatoes, peeled
- 12 carrot, (7-1/2")s carrots, chopped
- 1 cup chopped onion
- 1 tablespoon canola oil
- 1 (3 pound) boneless beef chuck roast
- 1 (15 ounce) can tomato sauce
- ¼ cup packed brown sugar
- 2 tablespoons Worcestershire sauce, or more to taste
- 2 tablespoons cider vinegar
- 1 teaspoon salt

Directions

Step 1

Combine potatoes, carrots, and onion in the bottom of a slow cooker.

Step 2

Heat canola oil in a large skillet over medium-high heat. Cook beef roast in the hot oil until browned completely, 2 to 3 minutes per side; place beef roast atop the vegetables.

Step 3

Stir tomato sauce, brown sugar, Worcestershire sauce, cider vinegar, and salt together in a bowl; pour over the roast.

Step 4

Cook on Low for 10 to 12 hours (or on High for 5 to 6 hours).

Step 5

Remove roast and vegetables to a serving platter. Pour sauce into skillet and cook over medium-high heat until thickened, 5 to 10 minutes; serve with the beef and vegetables.

Nutrition Facts

Per Serving:

529.6 calories; protein 36.9g 74% DV; carbohydrates 59.9g 19% DV; fat 16.2g 25% DV; cholesterol 105.3mg 35% DV; sodium 993.9mg 40% DV.

Oven Stew

Prep: 15 mins **Cook:** 2 hrs 30 mins **Total:** 2 hrs 45 mins

Servings: 5

Yield: 4 to 6 servings

Ingredients

- ¼ cup all-purpose flour
- 2 pounds cubed stew meat
- 2 tablespoons vegetable oil
- 1 (14.5 ounce) can stewed tomatoes
- 5 medium (blank)s carrots, chopped
- 3 medium (2-1/4" to 3" dia, raw)s potatoes - peeled and cubed
- ½ (10 ounce) package frozen peas
- 1 ½ cups water
- 1 (1 ounce) package dry onion soup mix
- 1 teaspoon salt
- ¼ teaspoon ground black pepper

Directions

Step 1

Preheat oven to 400 degrees F (200 degrees C).

Step 2

Place the flour in a large resealable plastic bag. Pour in the meat, seal the bag and shake well to coat. Spread the oil in the bottom of a 10x15 inch roasting pan, then arrange the meat in a single layer in the pan.

Step 3

Bake at 400 degrees F (200 degrees C) for 30 minutes.

Step 4

Remove from oven and add the tomatoes, carrots, potatoes, peas, water, onion soup mix, salt and ground black pepper. Stir with a wooden spoon, cover and return to the oven.

Step 5

Reduce oven temperature to 375 degrees F (190 degrees C) for 1 1/2 to 2 hours, or to desired tenderness.

Nutrition Facts

Per Serving:

708.4 calories; protein 39.5g 79% DV; carbohydrates 45.4g 15% DV; fat 41.1g 63% DV; cholesterol 121.6mg 41% DV; sodium 1322.7mg 53% DV.

Smoked Sausage Skillet Pot Pie

Prep: 20 mins **Cook:** 10 mins **Total:** 30 mins

Servings: 6

Yield: 6 servings

Ingredients

- 1 (14 ounce) package Hillshire Farm Smoked Sausage, diagonally cut into 1/4-inch slices
- 1 medium onion, 1/2-inch dice
- 3 medium (blank)s carrots, 1/2 inch dice
- 3 stalks celery, 1/2-inch dice
- 1 teaspoon dried thyme
- 3 tablespoons all-purpose flour
- 1 cup chicken broth
- 1 teaspoon Worcestershire sauce
- ¼ teaspoon salt
- 1 sheet refrigerated pie crust
- 1 egg, beaten

Directions

Step 1

Preheat oven to 450 degrees F.

Step 2

Heat a 10-inch oven-proof skillet over medium-high heat and add smoked sausage, stirring occasionally until browned, 6 - 9 minutes.

Step 3

Reduce heat to medium and add onion, carrot, celery and thyme. Continue to cook until the vegetables are soft, about 5 minutes. Mix in the flour then add the broth, Worcestershire sauce and salt. Cook until mixture is thick and bubbly, 5 - 6 minutes.

Step 4

Turn off heat and work quickly to place the cold pie crust over the pan and fold the excess dough inward. Cut a steam vent in the center of the pie. Brush with the beaten egg and bake for 10 - 12 min until crust is golden brown.

Nutrition Facts

Per Serving:

440.7 calories; protein 12.4g 25% DV; carbohydrates 27.1g 9% DV; fat 30.8g 47% DV; cholesterol 72.3mg 24% DV; sodium 893.1mg 36% DV.

Auto Parts Chicken

Servings: 5

Yield: 5 servings

Ingredients

- 1 tablespoon butter
- 1 tablespoon olive oil
- 4 breast half, bone and skin removed (blank)s skinless, boneless chicken breasts
- 2 cloves garlic, minced
- 1 leek, chopped
- ½ white onion, sliced into thin wedges
- 4 large potatoes, chopped
- 2 large carrots, sliced diagonally
- 1 (10.75 ounce) can herb seasoned chicken broth
- ⅔ cup water
- 1 bay leaf, crushed
- ground black pepper to taste
- 2 teaspoons dried parsley
- 2 tablespoons all-purpose flour
- 2 tablespoons water

Directions

Step 1

In a large skillet, heat the butter/margarine and oil over medium heat. Lightly brown the chicken breast halves. Add the garlic, leek and onion and saute until they begin to soften. Add the potatoes and carrots, then add chicken broth, water, bay leaf, pepper and parsley. Simmer all together for 30 minutes or until vegetables are soft.

Step 2

Combine 2 tablespoons each flour and water and mix together (done easily if you shake together in a jar). Turn up heat under skillet and add flour/water mixture to thicken the juices.

Nutrition Facts

Per Serving:

435.2 calories; protein 31.3g 63% DV; carbohydrates 61.2g 20% DV; fat 7.3g 11% DV; cholesterol 60.9mg 20% DV; sodium 497.8mg 20% DV.

Easy Weeknight Tuna Pot Pie

Prep: 10 mins **Cook:** 20 mins **Additional:** 5 mins **Total:** 35 mins

Servings: 8

Yield: 8 servings

Ingredients

- 2 tablespoons butter
- 1 small onion, diced
- 2 (5 ounce) cans tuna, drained
- 1 (10 ounce) package frozen mixed vegetables
- 1 (10.75 ounce) can condensed cream of mushroom soup
- ½ cup shredded Cheddar cheese
- 1 (8 ounce) package refrigerated crescent rolls

Directions

Step 1

Preheat an oven to 350 degrees F (175 degrees C).

Step 2

Melt the butter in a saucepan over medium heat. Add onions and cook until soft and translucent. Mix in the tuna and frozen vegetables, stirring often until the vegetables are heated through, 5 to 10 minutes. Stir in the cream of mushroom soup. Pour the tuna mixture into a 9 inch pie dish and sprinkle with shredded cheese.

Step 3

Unroll and separate the crescent rolls. Lay each crescent roll on top of the tuna mixture with the point facing inward, the rolls may overlap slightly. Bake until crescent rolls are golden brown and mixture is bubbly, 11 to 13 minutes. Let the pie sit for 5 to 10 minutes before cutting and serving.

Nutrition Facts

Per Serving:

265.6 calories; protein 14.1g 28% DV; carbohydrates 19.3g 6% DV; fat 14.4g 22% DV; cholesterol 26.1mg 9% DV; sodium 572.5mg 23% DV.

Grandma Earhart's Pepper Pot Casserole

Prep: 25 mins **Cook:** 50 mins **Total:** 1 hr 15 mins

Servings: 6

Yield: 6 servings

Ingredients

- 1 tablespoon vegetable oil
- 2 tablespoons butter
- 1 onion, chopped
- ½ cup sliced celery
- ½ green bell pepper, chopped
- 1 pound bulk pork sausage
- 1 (28 ounce) can whole peeled tomatoes, chopped
- ½ teaspoon garlic powder
- 1 teaspoon dried basil
- ½ teaspoon dried sage
- 1 tablespoon Worcestershire sauce
- 1 (8 ounce) package egg noodles
- 1 cup grated Cheddar cheese

Directions

Step 1

Preheat oven to 350 degrees F (175 degrees C).

Step 2

Heat the vegetable oil with butter in a large skillet over medium heat, and cook the onion, celery, and green pepper until the vegetables are tender, stirring occasionally, about 8 minutes. Mix in the pork sausage, and cook until the meat is browned, breaking it up into crumbles as it cooks, about 8 more minutes. Drain off excess grease. Stir in the tomatoes, garlic powder, basil, sage, and Worcestershire sauce, mixing until well combined.

Step 3

Fill a large pot with lightly salted water and bring to a rolling boil over high heat. Once the water is boiling, stir in the egg noodles, and return to a boil. Cook the pasta uncovered, stirring occasionally, until the pasta has cooked through, but is still firm to the bite, about 5 minutes. Drain well in a colander set in the sink. Mix the noodles gently into the pork mixture, and place into a 9x12-inch baking dish. Sprinkle the top with Cheddar cheese.

Step 4

Bake in the preheated oven until the cheese is bubbling and browned, 30 to 40 minutes.

Nutrition Facts

Per Serving:

510.3 calories; protein 21.9g 44% DV; carbohydrates 37.7g 12% DV; fat 30.5g 47% DV; cholesterol 104.6mg 35% DV; sodium 1051.7mg 42% DV.

Slow Cooker Savory Pot Roast

Prep: 10 mins **Cook:** 8 hrs **Total:** 8 hrs 10 mins

Servings: 6

Yield: 6 servings

Ingredients

- 1 (10.75 ounce) can Condensed Cream of Mushroom Soup (Regular, 98% Fat Free or Healthy Request)
- 1 (2 ounce) pouch Campbell's Dry Onion Soup and Recipe Mix
- 6 small red potatoes, halved
- 6 medium carrots, cut into 2-inch pieces
- 1 (3 pound) boneless beef bottom round roast or chuck pot roast

Directions

Step 1

Stir the soup, onion soup mix, potatoes and carrots in a 4 1/2-quart slow cooker. Add the beef and turn to coat.

Step 2

Cover and cook on LOW for 8 to 9 hours* or until the beef is fork-tender.

Nutrition Facts

Per Serving:

683.4 calories; protein 50g 100% DV; carbohydrates 42g 14% DV; fat 33.3g 51% DV; cholesterol 147.1mg 49% DV; sodium 1356.9mg 54% DV.

Mashed Potato-Topped Turkey Pot Pie

Prep: 20 mins **Cook:** 45 mins **Total:** 1 hr 5 mins

Servings: 6

Yield: 1 9x13-inch pan

Ingredients

- 1 pastry for a single pie crust
- 4 cups cubed cooked turkey
- 1 (10.75 ounce) can condensed cream of chicken soup
- 2 cups water, divided
- 2 (1.2 ounce) packages turkey gravy mix
- 1 (16 ounce) package frozen mixed vegetables
- 4 cups mashed potatoes

Directions

Step 1

Preheat oven to 375 degrees F (190 degrees C).

Step 2

Press the pie crust into the bottom of a 9x13-inch baking dish, then layer the turkey meat over the crust; spoon the cream of chicken soup over the turkey.

Step 3

Bring 1 cup of water to a boil in a saucepan over medium heat, and stir in the mixed vegetables; cook until the vegetables are tender, about 5 minutes. Whisk the dry gravy mix with the remaining 1 cup of water, then stir the gravy mixture into the mixed vegetables. Bring to a boil, then simmer until thickened, about 1 minute. Pour the vegetables and gravy over the cream of chicken soup layer in the pan. Spread the mashed potatoes over the top of the pie.

Step 4

Bake in the preheated oven until the filling is bubbling, about 45 minutes.

Nutrition Facts

Per Serving:

561.7 calories; protein 36.6g 73% DV; carbohydrates 60.2g 19% DV; fat 19.2g 30% DV; cholesterol 79mg 26% DV; sodium 1398.7mg 56% DV.

Apple Cider Pepper Pot Roast (Pressure Cooker Recipe)

Prep: 15 mins **Cook:** 1 hr 1 min **Total:** 1 hr 16 mins

Servings: 8

Yield: 8 servings

Ingredients

- 1 large red onion, quartered
- 4 stalks celery, cut into large chunks
- 8 eaches baby carrots
- 4 ounces mushrooms, halved, or more to taste
- 6 cloves garlic
- 1 (2 1/2 pound) beef chuck pot roast
- ¼ cup olive oil, divided
- kosher salt to taste
- ground black pepper
- ¼ cup sweet red wine
- 1 cup beef broth
- ⅓ cup apple cider
- 6 sprigs fresh thyme
- 4 eaches fresh bay leaves

Directions

Step 1

Place onion, celery, baby carrots, mushrooms, and garlic in a food processor; pulse to coarsely chop.

Step 2

Coat roast generously with 2 tablespoons olive oil; season both sides with salt and black pepper.

Step 3

Heat remaining 2 tablespoons olive oil in a pressure cooker over medium heat. Cook roast until browned, 2 to 3 minutes per side. Transfer roast to a large plate.

Step 4

Place chopped vegetable mixture in the pressure cooker; cook and stir until slightly softened, about 2 minutes. Stir in wine and cook until flavors combine, about 1 minute. Pour in broth and apple cider. Stir in thyme and bay leaves into sauce. Place roast back in the cooker; spoon sauce to cover roast as much as possible.

Step 5

Cover and cook at high pressure according to manufacturer's instructions, 50 to 60 minutes. Remove from heat and allow pressure to release naturally according to manufacturer's instructions.

Nutrition Facts

Per Serving:

299.8 calories; protein 18.2g 36% DV; carbohydrates 5.4g 2% DV; fat 22g 34% DV; cholesterol 64.6mg 22% DV; sodium 208.7mg 8% DV.

Puff Pastry Roast Beef Pot Pies

Prep: 25 mins **Cook:** 1 hr **Total:** 1 hr 25 mins

Servings: 6

Yield: 6 servings

Ingredients

- 1 tablespoon olive oil
- 2 cups cubed beef stew meat
- 1 onion, diced
- 2 eaches yellow potatoes, peeled and diced
- 2 carrot, (7-1/2")s carrots, diced
- 1 rib celery, diced

- 1 clove garlic, crushed
- ¼ cup all-purpose flour
- 2 tablespoons butter
- 1 bay leaf
- salt and ground black pepper to taste
- 3 cups low-sodium beef stock
- 1 cup milk
- 1 sprig fresh rosemary
- ½ cup frozen peas
- 1 (17.5 ounce) package frozen puff pastry, thawed

Directions

Step 1

Preheat oven to 350 degrees F (175 degrees C).

Step 2

Heat olive oil in a large stockpot over medium heat; cook and stir stew meat until browned, 2 to 3 minutes. Add onion; cook and stir until onion is lightly browned, 3 to 4 minutes. Add potatoes, carrots, celery, and garlic; cook and stir until slightly tender, 3 to 4 minutes.

Step 3

Stir flour, butter, bay leaf, salt, and pepper into stew meat mixture; cook and stir until flour is dissolved and a gravy is forming, about 2 minutes. Pour beef stock over meat mixture, scraping brown bits of food off the bottom with a wooden spoon; cook until gravy begins to thicken, about 5 minutes.

Step 4

Mix milk and rosemary into stew meat-gravy mixture; continue cooking over low heat for 15 to 20 minutes. Stir peas into mixture.

Step 5

Pour stew meat-gravy mixture into individual pot pie pans or a 12-inch cast iron skillet; top with puff pastry, crimping the sides of the pastry down tightly. Cover with aluminum foil.

Step 6

Bake in the preheated oven until pastry is puffed and golden, 30 to 45 minutes.

Nutrition Facts

Per Serving:

833.7 calories; protein 30.3g 61% DV; carbohydrates 59.7g 19% DV; fat 52.4g 81% DV; cholesterol 75.8mg 25% DV; sodium 423.6mg 17% DV.

Cyndee's Best Slow Cooker Italian Pot Roast

Prep: 20 mins **Cook:** 8 hrs **Total:** 8 hrs 20 mins

Servings: 6

Yield: 6 servings

Ingredients

- 3 ½ pounds top round steak
- 1 large onion, diced
- 2 stalk (blank)s celery ribs, finely chopped
- 1 red bell pepper, seeded and diced
- 1 green bell pepper, seeded and diced
- 1 (1 ounce) packet dry au jus mix
- 4 cups water, or amount to cover

Add All **Ingredients** To Shopping List

Directions

Instructions Checklist

Step 1

Place the pot roast in a slow cooker. Add the onion, celery, red and green bell peppers, au jus mix, and enough water to cover the meat. Cover and cook on Low for 8 hours, or until tender.

I Made It Print

Nutrition Facts

Per Serving:

503.8 calories; protein 57.7g 115% DV; carbohydrates 8g 3% DV; fat 25g 38% DV; cholesterol 161.4mg 54% DV; sodium 688.1mg 28% DV.

To-Die-For Chicken Pot Pie

Prep: 45 mins **Cook:** 1 hr **Total:** 1 hr 45 mins

Servings: 6

Yield: 1 pot pie

Ingredients

- 6 medium (blank)s carrots, chopped
- 6 stalks celery, chopped
- 1 cup fresh or frozen peas
- 1 cup fresh or frozen green beans, thawed
- 1 cup corn kernels
- 1 yellow onion, diced
- 1 cup quartered red potatoes
- 3 cups chicken broth
- 1 teaspoon thyme
- ½ teaspoon salt
- ½ teaspoon ground black pepper
- 4 (.87 ounce) packages dry chicken gravy mix
- 4 cups water
- 1 (15 ounce) package double crust ready-to-use pie crusts (such as Pillsbury)
- 1 whole roasted chicken, bones and skin removed, meat shredded
- ¼ cup butter, cut into pieces
- 1 egg
- ¼ cup milk

Directions

Step 1

Preheat oven to 425 degrees F (220 degrees C). Place a baking sheet on the a rack on which you'll bake the pie.

Step 2

Combine the carrots, celery, peas, green beans, corn, onion, red potatoes, and chicken broth in a large pot. Season the vegetable mixture with thyme, salt, and black pepper; bring to a boil. Reduce heat to medium-low, cover, and simmer until the vegetables are tender, about 15 minutes. Drain the vegetables and set aside.

Step 3

Place dry chicken gravy mix into another saucepan and gradually whisk in the water until smooth. Bring the mixture to a boil, reduce heat to medium-low, and simmer until thickened, about 1 minute. Set gravy aside and allow to continue to thicken as it cools.

Step 4

Press one of the pie crusts into the bottom of a 9-inch pie dish. Spoon a layer of gravy (about 1/3 cup) into the crust. Layer the cooked vegetables and shredded chicken into the crust until the filling is level with the top of the pie dish. Pour the rest of the gravy slowly over the filling until gravy is visible at the top. Scatter butter pieces over the filling; top with second crust. Seal the 2 crusts together and crimp with a fork.

Step 5

Whisk the egg and milk together in a bowl, and brush the egg wash over the top crust. Pierce the top crust several times to vent steam.

Step 6

Bake the pot pie in the preheated oven until the filling is bubbling and the crust is golden brown, about 45 minutes to 1 hour. Check periodically to see if the edge of the crust is browning too quickly; if needed, cover the edge with a strip of aluminum foil to prevent over-browning.

Nutrition Facts

Per Serving:

677.5 calories; protein 25.2g 50% DV; carbohydrates 64.5g 21% DV; fat 37.7g 58% DV; cholesterol 101.6mg 34% DV; sodium 2154.4mg 86% DV.

Chicken and Biscuit Casserole

Prep: 30 mins **Cook:** 40 mins **Total:** 1 hr 10 mins

Servings: 6

Yield: 6 servings

Ingredients

- ¼ cup butter
- 2 cloves garlic, minced
- ½ cup chopped onion
- ½ cup chopped celery
- ½ cup chopped baby carrots
- ½ cup all-purpose flour
- 2 teaspoons white sugar
- 1 teaspoon salt
- 1 teaspoon dried basil
- ½ teaspoon ground black pepper
- 4 cups chicken broth
- 1 (10 ounce) can peas, drained
- 4 cups diced, cooked chicken meat
- 2 cups buttermilk baking mix

- 2 teaspoons dried basil
- ⅔ cup milk

Directions

Step 1

Preheat oven to 350 degrees F (175 degrees C). Lightly grease a 9x13 inch baking dish.

Step 2

In a skillet, melt the butter over medium-high heat. Cook and stir the garlic, onion, celery, and carrots in butter until tender. Mix in the flour, sugar, salt, 1 teaspoon dried basil, and pepper. Stir in broth, and bring to a boil. Stirring constantly, boil 1 minute, reduce heat, and stir in peas. Simmer 5 minutes, then mix in chicken. Transfer mixture to the prepared baking dish.

Step 3

In a medium bowl, combine the baking mix and 2 teaspoons dried basil. Stir in milk to form a dough. Divide the dough into 6 to 8 balls. On floured wax paper, use the palm of your hand to flatten each ball of dough into a circular shape; place on top of chicken mixture.

Step 4

Bake in the preheated oven for 30 minutes. Cover with foil, and bake for 10 more minutes. To serve, spoon chicken mixture over biscuits.

Nutrition Facts

Per Serving:

450.5 calories; protein 33.5g 67% DV; carbohydrates 48g 16% DV; fat 13.2g 20% DV; cholesterol 95.8mg 32% DV; sodium 2014.6mg 81% DV.

Healthier (but still awesome) Awesome Slow Cooker Pot Roast

Prep: 10 mins **Cook:** 8 hrs **Total:** 8 hrs 10 mins

Servings: 12

Yield: 12 servings

Ingredients

- 2 (10.75 ounce) cans low-fat, low-sodium condensed cream of mushroom soup
- 1 large onion, chopped
- 3 pounds chuck roast
- 2 cups sliced carrots
- 1 pound small red potatoes
- ½ pound string beans
- ¼ cup chopped parsley

Directions

Step 1

Mix cream of mushroom soup, chopped onion, and chuck roast in a slow cooker.

Step 2

Cook on High for 3 to 4 hours, or on Low for 8 to 9 hours. Add carrots, potatoes, string beans, and parsley 1 1/2 hours before the pot roast done.

Nutrition Facts

Per Serving:

304.8 calories; protein 24.1g 48% DV; carbohydrates 14.7g 5% DV; fat 16.2g 25% DV; cholesterol 75.7mg 25% DV; sodium 298.6mg 12% DV.

Easy Peach Crisp

Prep: 10 mins **Cook:** 25 mins **Total:** 35 mins

Servings: 12

Yield: 12 servings

Ingredients

- 1 (29 ounce) can sliced peaches, with juice
- 1 (18.25 ounce) package yellow cake mix
- ½ cup margarine
- 1 cup white sugar
- 1 teaspoon ground cinnamon

Directions

Step 1

Preheat oven to 350 degrees F (175 degrees C).

Step 2

Pour canned peaches into a 9x13 inch baking pan; make sure juices cover peaches, if not add a small amount of water to just cover fruit. Mix peaches with 1/2 cup of the sugar and sprinkle cinnamon to taste into mixture.

Step 3

Sprinkle dry cake mix evenly over top of peach mixture. Poke holes into cake mix to allow juice through. Cut stick of margarine into small pats, placing randomly over the top. Sprinkle with the remaining 1/2 cup of sugar and a light dusting of cinnamon.

Step 4

Bake in preheated oven for 25 to 30 minutes, or until the juice mixture is bubbly and the top of the cake mix topping is crusty and golden brown.

Nutrition Facts

Per Serving:

347.7 calories; protein 2.4g 5% DV; carbohydrates 58.4g 19% DV; fat 12.5g 19% DV; cholesterol 0.9mg; sodium 373.4mg 15% DV.

Turkey Spaghetti Zoodles

Prep: 15 mins **Cook:** 9 mins **Total:** 24 mins

Servings: 5

Yield: 5 servings

Ingredients

- 1 teaspoon extra-virgin olive oil
- 1 ¼ pounds ground turkey breast
- 1 cup diced green bell pepper
- 1 tablespoon minced garlic
- 2 teaspoons Italian seasoning
- ½ teaspoon ground black pepper
- ¼ teaspoon salt
- ¼ teaspoon red pepper flakes
- 3 cups marinara sauce
- 2 cups baby spinach leaves
- 4 eaches zucchini, cut into noodle-shape strands

Directions

Step 1

Heat olive oil in a large skillet over medium heat. Add turkey breast, green pepper, garlic, Italian seasoning, ground black pepper, salt, and red pepper flakes; cook and stir until turkey is lightly browned, 4 to 5 minutes.

Step 2

Stir marinara sauce and baby spinach into the turkey mixture; cook and stir until marinara sauce is warm through, about 3 minutes.

Step 3

Stir zucchini noodles into the sauce with tongs; cook and stir until the zucchini is slightly tender, 2 to 3 minutes.

Nutrition Facts

Per Serving:

301.2 calories; protein 34.3g 69% DV; carbohydrates 26.8g 9% DV; fat 6.1g 9% DV; cholesterol 84.8mg 28% DV; sodium 802.9mg 32% DV.

Zucchini Noodle Primavera

Prep: 20 mins **Cook:** 14 mins **Additional:** 20 mins **Total:** 54 mins

Servings: 2

Yield: 2 servings

Ingredients

- 1 zucchini, or more to taste
- 1 teaspoon salt, or as needed
- ¼ cup olive oil
- 1 small onion, thinly sliced lengthwise
- ½ red bell pepper, cut into matchstick-sized pieces
- 1 cup yellow grape tomatoes
- ½ teaspoon garlic powder
- 2 tablespoons milk, or more to taste
- ½ cup grated pecorino cheese
- ½ teaspoon ground black pepper
- ½ teaspoon dried oregano

Directions

Step 1

Cut zucchini into noodle shapes with a spiralizer; toss with salt until combined. Drain on a paper towel until moisture is drawn out; about 20 minutes. Squeeze zucchini noodles to remove remaining moisture.

Step 2

Heat olive oil in a skillet over medium heat. Add onion and red bell pepper; cook and stir until onion is soft and translucent, about 5 minutes. Stir in tomatoes and cook until soft, 3 to 4 minutes.

Step 3

Stir zucchini into the onion mixture; cook and stir until tender and mixture looks dry, about 5 minutes. Sprinkle with garlic powder. Stir in milk and cook, 1 to 2 minutes. Add pecorino cheese, pepper, and oregano; stir until combined.

Nutrition Facts

Per Serving:

399.4 calories; protein 10.7g 22% DV; carbohydrates 12.3g 4% DV; fat 33.8g 52% DV; cholesterol 21.2mg 7% DV; sodium 1545.2mg 62% DV.

Chicken and Rice with Cumin and Cilantro

Prep: 30 mins **Cook:** 53 mins **Total:** 1 hr 23 mins

Servings: 8

Yield: 8 servings

Ingredients

- 2 tablespoons olive oil
- 20 eaches chicken wings, tips removed and sections separated
- 2 ½ cups coarsely chopped onions
- ¼ cup coarsely chopped garlic
- ¼ cup chopped peeled ginger
- 2 cups long-grain white rice
- 1 ½ tablespoons ground cumin
- 2 ½ cups water
- 2 cups chopped cilantro stems, divided
- 1 (14 ounce) can diced tomatoes
- 1 tablespoon sriracha sauce
- 2 ½ teaspoons salt

Directions

Step 1

Heat olive oil in a pot large enough to hold chicken wings in a single layer. Add chicken wings; cook until browned, about 8 minutes. Turn wings with tongs; cook until second side is browned, about 8 minutes more. Transfer to a bowl using tongs.

Step 2

Stir onions, garlic, and ginger into the drippings in the pot; cook until fragrant, 2 to 3 minutes. Stir in rice and cumin. Add water, 1 1/2 cup cilantro stems, tomatoes, sriracha sauce, and salt.

Step 3

Return wings to the pot. Bring broth to a boil. Cover, reduce heat to low, and simmer until rice and wings are tender, about 30 minutes. Garnish with remaining 1/2 cup cilantro stems.

Nutrition Facts

Per Serving:

388.4 calories; protein 18.1g 36% DV; carbohydrates 46.3g 15% DV; fat 13.8g 21% DV; cholesterol 40.3mg 13% DV; sodium 937.4mg 38% DV.

Chocolate Tahini Pudding

Prep: 5 mins **Cook:** 10 mins **Total:** 15 mins

Servings: 4

Yield: 4 servings

Ingredients

- ½ cup white sugar
- 3 tablespoons unsweetened cocoa powder
- 2 tablespoons cornstarch
- ⅛ teaspoon salt
- 2 ¾ cups milk
- 1 tablespoon tahini
- 1 teaspoon vanilla extract

Directions

Step 1

Mix sugar, cocoa powder, cornstarch, and salt together in a saucepan. Stir in milk. Bring to a boil over medium heat and cook, stirring constantly, until mixture thickens and coats the back of a spoon, about 5 minutes. Remove from heat. Add tahini and vanilla extract; stir well.

Nutrition Facts

Per Serving:

230.6 calories; protein 7g 14% DV; carbohydrates 39.6g 13% DV; fat 5.9g 9% DV; cholesterol 13.4mg 5% DV; sodium 147.1mg 6% DV.

Taiwanese Ground Pork and Pickled Cucumbers

Prep: 15 mins **Cook:** 17 mins **Total:** 32 mins

Servings: 2

Yield: 2 servings

Ingredients

Seasoning:

- 1 tablespoon Chinese rice wine
- 1 tablespoon soy sauce paste
- 1 tablespoon soy sauce
- 1 teaspoon white sugar
- 3 dashes ground white pepper
- ½ pound ground pork
- ⅓ cup Taiwanese pickled cucumbers with brine, chopped
- 1 tablespoon vegetable oil
- 2 small shallots, thinly sliced
- 2 cloves garlic, minced
- 1 teaspoon minced fresh ginger
- ¼ teaspoon ground star anise
- 1 ½ cups water
- ¼ teaspoon sesame oil
- 2 eaches green onions, chopped

Directions

Step 1

Mix rice wine, soy sauce paste, soy sauce, sugar, and white pepper together in a bowl.

Step 2

Mix ground pork with brine from cucumbers together in a bowl.

Step 3

Heat oil in a large skillet over medium heat. Add shallots; cook and stir until golden brown, about 5 minutes. Add pork mixture; cook and stir until no longer pink, 3 to 4 minutes. Push pork and shallots to the sides of the skillet, making a space in the center. Add garlic, ginger, and star anise; stir.

Step 4

Pour water into the skillet; bring to a boil. Reduce heat to medium low; simmer until sauce reduces to about 1 cup. Stir in chopped cucumbers. Stir in rice wine mixture; cook until flavors combine, 4 to 6 minutes.

Step 5

Top pork mixture with sesame oil and green onions.

Cook's Note:

Substitute 1/8 teaspoon Chinese Five-Spice powder for the ground star anise if desired.

Nutrition Facts

Per Serving:

356.2 calories; protein 22.3g 45% DV; carbohydrates 11g 4% DV; fat 23.8g 37% DV; cholesterol 73.3mg 24% DV; sodium 1282mg 51% DV.

Boeuf Bourguignon

Prep: 20 mins **Cook:** 2 hrs 14 mins **Total:** 2 hrs 34 mins

Servings: 8

Yield: 8 servings

Ingredients

- ¼ cup vegetable oil
- 5 eaches onions, sliced
- 2 pounds lean beef, cut into 1-inch cubes
- 1 ½ tablespoons all-purpose flour
- ¼ teaspoon dried marjoram
- ¼ teaspoon dried thyme
- freshly ground black pepper to taste
- 1 cup dry red wine
- ½ cup beef broth

- 1 (8 ounce) package sliced fresh mushrooms

Directions

Step 1

Heat oil in a large, heavy skillet over medium heat. Add onions; cook and stir until tender, about 10 minutes. Transfer to a bowl.

Step 2

Cook and stir beef in the same skillet until browned, 1 to 2 minutes per side. Sprinkle flour, marjoram, thyme, and pepper over beef. Pour red wine and beef broth into the skillet; stir well. Reduce heat to low and simmer until beef is tender, 1 1/2 to 2 hours.

Step 3

Stir onions into the skillet. Add mushrooms. Cook, stirring, until mushrooms are tender and sauce is thick and dark brown, about 30 minutes.

Cook's Notes:

Substitute olive oil for the vegetable oil if desired.

Add beef broth and wine (1 part broth to 2 parts wine) as needed in **step 2** to keep beef barely covered.

Nutrition Facts

Per Serving:

350.2 calories; protein 19.7g 40% DV; carbohydrates 16.2g 5% DV; fat 20.7g 32% DV; cholesterol 57.7mg 19% DV; sodium 97.3mg 4% DV.

Coconut Red Lentil Curry

Prep: 30 mins **Cook:** 39 mins **Total:** 1 hr 9 mins

Servings: 6

Yield: 6 servings

Ingredients

- 2 tablespoons Pure Wesson Canola Oil, divided
- 1 large head cauliflower, cut into small florets
- 1 cup chopped onion
- 1 teaspoon minced garlic
- 1 tablespoon grated fresh ginger
- 1 teaspoon ground cumin
- 1 teaspoon ground turmeric
- ½ teaspoon ground coriander
- 1 teaspoon salt
- 2 peppers (2 1/2-inch) serrano peppers, finely chopped with seeds
- 1 ½ cups dry red lentils, sorted and rinsed
- 1 (14.5 ounce) can Hunt's Diced Tomatoes, drained
- 2 cups vegetable broth
- 1 (13.5 ounce) can coconut milk
- ½ cup diced carrot
- 1 cup frozen green peas

Directions

Step 1

In a deep 12-inch skillet, heat 1 tablespoon oil over medium-high heat. Add cauliflower and cook 3 minutes, stirring occasionally, until lightly browned; set aside.

Step 2

Reduce heat to medium and add remaining oil. Sauté onion 2 minutes until soft. Add garlic and ginger and cook, stirring, 1 minute. Add cumin, turmeric, coriander, salt and serrano peppers; stir well and cook 1 minute or until spices are fragrant. Add lentils, stir well to coat. Stir in diced tomatoes and broth; bring to a boil. Cover and reduce heat to medium-low, simmer 12 minutes.

Step 3

Stir in coconut milk, carrots and cauliflower. Simmer 10 minutes. Add peas and continue to simmer 5 minutes. If desired, top with chopped cilantro and serve with yogurt and warm naan bread.

Nutrition Facts

Per Serving:

425.3 calories; protein 19.3g 39% DV; carbohydrates 48.5g 16% DV; fat 19.9g 31% DV; cholesterolmg; sodium 849.7mg 34% DV.

Vanilla Sesame Cake

Prep: 30 mins **Cook:** 40 mins **Additional:** 30 mins **Total:** 1 hr 40 mins

Servings: 12

Yield: 1 9x13-inch cake

Ingredients

- 1 ⅛ cups butter, softened
- 1 ¼ cups white sugar
- 6 large eggs eggs
- 1 tablespoon vanilla extract
- ⅔ cup black sesame seeds
- 2 cups self-rising flour

Directions

Step 1

Preheat oven to 350 degrees F (175 degrees C). Grease and flour a 9x13-inch baking dish.

Step 2

With an electric mixer, beat the butter and sugar together in a mixing bowl until the mixture is creamy, about 5 minutes. Beat in the eggs, one at a time, beating until each egg is incorporated before adding the next one. Stir in the vanilla extract and black sesame seeds, mixing until well blended. Lightly stir in the flour to make a smooth batter, and pour the mixture into the prepared baking dish.

Step 3

Bake in the preheated oven until a toothpick inserted into the center of the cake comes out clean, about 40 minutes. Cool in the pans for 10 minutes before removing to cool completely on a wire rack.

Nutrition Facts

Per Serving:

390.5 calories; protein 6.8g 14% DV; carbohydrates 38.5g 12% DV; fat 23.9g 37% DV; cholesterol 138.8mg 46% DV; sodium 422.3mg 17% DV.

Chicken Stuff

Servings: 6

Yield: 6 servings

Ingredients

- 4 breast half, bone and skin removed (blank)s boneless skinless chicken breasts, cut into 1 inch pieces
- 1 cup butter
- 2 (10.75 ounce) cans condensed cream of mushroom soup
- 2 cups macaroni
- 1 pinch garlic salt
- ¼ teaspoon lemon pepper
- 1 cup sliced fresh mushrooms

Directions

Step 1

In a large skillet, melt butter or margarine over medium heat. Lay chicken strips in butter or margarine, and sprinkle with garlic salt and lemon pepper. Cook, turning frequently, until chicken strips are golden brown on all sides; the chicken should be still soft, not fried hard. Stack cooked strips at outer edges of the skillet if you need to cook more strips.

Step 2

When all chicken strips are browned, add condensed mushroom soup, 1 soup can of water, and mushrooms to skillet; blend well with pan drippings and chicken strips. Add macaroni noodles, and just enough water to cover noodles; stir well. Lower heat, and cover. Simmer until noodles are done, stirring frequently.

Nutrition Facts

Per Serving:

576.8 calories; protein 25.1g 50% DV; carbohydrates 33.4g 11% DV; fat 38.2g 59% DV; cholesterol 127mg 42% DV; sodium 1001.6mg 40% DV.

Spicy Spanish Sausage Supper

Prep: 30 mins **Cook:** 30 mins **Total:** 1 hr

Servings: 4

Yield: 4 servings

Ingredients

- ½ cup chopped green bell pepper
- ⅓ cup chopped celery
- ¼ cup chopped onion
- 1 tablespoon vegetable oil
- 1 pound smoked sausage, sliced
- 2 cups water
- 1 (10 ounce) can diced tomatoes with green chile peppers
- 1 (6.8 ounce) package Spanish-style rice mix
- ¼ cup sliced stuffed green olives
- ⅛ teaspoon ground black pepper

Directions

Step 1

In a large skillet over medium heat, saute the green bell pepper, celery and onion in the oil for 5 to 10 minutes, or until tender.

Step 2

Add the sausage, water, tomatoes and green chiles, rice, olives and ground black pepper. Mix well and simmer for 20 minutes, stirring occasionally.

Nutrition Facts

Per Serving:

657.2 calories; protein 30.4g 61% DV; carbohydrates 41.2g 13% DV; fat 41.3g 64% DV; cholesterol 77.2mg 26% DV; sodium 3122.7mg 125% DV.

Pakistani Pot Roast Beef Fillets (Pasanday)

Prep: 15 mins **Cook:** 40 mins **Total:** 55 mins

Servings: 8

Yield: 8 servings

Ingredients

- 1 cup plain yogurt
- 1 teaspoon ginger garlic paste
- 2 teaspoons crushed red pepper flakes
- ½ teaspoon ground black cumin
- ½ teaspoon ground cloves
- ¼ teaspoon ground turmeric
- 2 teaspoons salt
- 2 pounds round steak, cut into pieces
- ¾ cup vegetable oil
- 1 medium onion, thinly sliced
- 1 ½ tablespoons lemon juice
- 1 bunch fresh cilantro, for garnish
- 4 peppers fresh green chilies, for garnish

Directions

Step 1

In a medium bowl, combine yogurt, ginger garlic paste, pepper flakes, cumin, cloves, turmeric and salt. Mix in beef until evenly coated. Set aside for 15 minutes.

Step 2

Heat oil in a large heavy skillet over medium-high heat. Fry onion until golden brown. Remove 1 tablespoon of onion, and set aside for garnish. Reduce heat to low. Place meat in skillet, cover, and cook until tender, about 25 minutes. Check every 10 minutes, and add water if necessary. Pour in lemon juice, and simmer for 10 minutes. Garnish with cilantro, green chiles, and reserved fried onion.

Nutrition Facts

Per Serving:

421.4 calories; protein 26.9g 54% DV; carbohydrates 6.7g 2% DV; fat 31.8g 49% DV; cholesterol 71mg 24% DV; sodium 687mg 28% DV.

Slow Cooker Chicken Pot Pie Stew

Prep: 20 mins **Cook:** 6 hrs **Total:** 6 hrs 20 mins

Servings: 16

Yield: 16 servings

Ingredients

- 4 large skinless, boneless chicken breast halves, cut into cubes
- 10 medium red potatoes, quartered
- 1 (8 ounce) package baby carrots
- 1 cup chopped celery
- 2 (26 ounce) cans condensed cream of chicken soup
- 6 cubes chicken bouillon
- 2 teaspoons garlic salt
- 1 teaspoon celery salt
- 1 tablespoon ground black pepper
- 1 (16 ounce) bag frozen mixed vegetables

Directions

Step 1

Combine the chicken, potatoes, carrots, celery, chicken soup, chicken bouillon, garlic salt, celery salt, and black pepper in a slow cooker; cook on High for 5 hours.

Step 2

Stir the frozen mixed vegetables into the slow cooker, and cook 1 hour more.

Nutrition Facts

Per Serving:

262.7 calories; protein 17.1g 34% DV; carbohydrates 33.7g 11% DV; fat 6.9g 11% DV; cholesterol 36.8mg 12% DV; sodium 1415.6mg 57% DV.

"Eat Them Right Out of the Pot" Vegetarian Collard Greens

Prep: 15 mins **Cook:** 3 hrs **Total:** 3 hrs 15 mins

Servings: 4

Yield: 4 servings

Ingredients

- 4 cups water, or as needed
- ¼ cup apple cider vinegar
- 1 tablespoon seafood seasoning (such as Old Bay)
- 1 tablespoon olive oil
- 1 bunch collard greens, trimmed and cut into 2-inch strips
- 2 small jalapeno peppers, diced
- 3 cloves garlic, halved lengthwise, or more to taste
- salt and ground black pepper to taste

Directions

Step 1

Fill a large stockpot halfway with water; add vinegar, seafood seasoning, and olive oil. Bring liquid to a boil.

Step 2

Mix collard greens, jalapeno peppers, and garlic into boiling water; return to a boil. Cover stockpot, reduce heat to medium-low, and simmer until greens are very tender, 3 to 4 hours.

Step 3

Drain water from greens and mash garlic cloves; season with salt and pepper.

Cook's Note:

You can easily prepare more collards than this - just make sure there is more water in your pot.

I also use my Cuisinart(R) Dutch oven to make these. Put all **ingredients** in Dutch oven about 1/3 full of water in a 250 degree F (121 degrees C) preheated oven for about 3 hours. Cover Dutch oven completely with lid. Check partway through cooking that more water isn't needed.

White vinegar or white wine vinegar can be used in place of apple cider vinegar.

Depending on your tolerance you can remove jalapeno peppers or you can dice them up and add to the collards (my favorite way).

Nutrition Facts

Per Serving:

59.4 calories; protein 2g 4% DV; carbohydrates 5.3g 2% DV; fat 3.7g 6% DV; cholesterolmg; sodium 438.5mg 18% DV.

Smothered Chicken Breasts

Prep: 5 mins **Cook:** 30 mins **Total:** 35 mins

Servings: 4

Yield: 4 servings

Ingredients

- 4 (6 ounce) skinless, boneless chicken breast halves
- ¼ teaspoon salt
- ¼ teaspoon lemon pepper seasoning
- 1 tablespoon vegetable oil
- 8 strips bacon
- 1 onion, sliced
- ¼ cup packed brown sugar
- ½ cup shredded Colby-Monterey Jack cheese

Directions

Step 1

Sprinkle chicken with salt and lemon-pepper.

Step 2

Heat oil in a large skillet over medium heat; cook the chicken breasts in hot oil until no longer pink in the center and the juices run clear, 13 to 15 minutes. An instant-read thermometer inserted into the center should read at least 165 degrees F (74 degrees C). Remove and keep warm.

Step 3

Place bacon in large skillet and cook over medium-high heat, turning occasionally, until evenly browned, about 10 minutes. Drain bacon slices on paper towels; reserve 2 tablespoons drippings. Cook and stir onion and brown sugar in reserved drippings until onion is golden, about 5 minutes.

Step 4

Place two bacon strips on each chicken breast half; top with caramelized onions and sprinkle with Colby-Monterey Jack cheese.

Nutrition Facts

Per Serving:

431.1 calories; protein 44g 88% DV; carbohydrates 16.9g 5% DV; fat 20.1g 31% DV; cholesterol 124.5mg 42% DV; sodium 809mg 32% DV.

Easy Classic Goulash

Prep: 20 mins **Cook:** 1 hr 5 mins **Total:** 1 hr 25 mins

Servings: 8

Yield: 8 servings

Ingredients

- 2 pounds lean ground beef
- 2 large yellow onions, chopped
- 6 cloves garlic, chopped
- 2 (15 ounce) cans tomato sauce
- 2 (14.5 ounce) cans diced tomatoes
- 3 cups water
- ½ cup sofrito sauce (such as Goya)
- 3 tablespoons Worcestershire sauce
- 2 tablespoons Italian seasoning
- 1 tablespoon seasoned salt, or to taste
- 3 eaches bay leaves
- 2 ½ cups uncooked elbow macaroni

Directions

Step 1

Heat a large pot or Dutch oven over medium-high heat. Cook and stir beef in the hot pot until browned and crumbly, about 10 minutes; drain and discard grease. Stir onion and garlic into beef; cook and stir until onion is translucent, about 10 minutes.

Step 2

Stir tomato sauce, diced tomatoes, water, sofrito, Worcestershire sauce, Italian seasoning, seasoned salt, and bay leaves into beef mixture. Bring mixture to a boil, reduce heat to low, cover the pot, and simmer, stirring occasionally, until flavors blend, about 20 minutes.

Step 3

Pour macaroni into beef mixture, cover the pot, and continue simmering until pasta is tender and flavors are completely blended, about 25 minutes. Discard bay leaves.

Nutrition Facts

Per Serving:

442.4 calories; protein 28.3g 57% DV; carbohydrates 41.5g 13% DV; fat 18.1g 28% DV; cholesterol 68.6mg 23% DV; sodium 1270.8mg 51% DV.

Chance's Chicken Spezzatino

Prep: 25 mins **Cook:** 35 mins **Additional:** 10 mins **Total:** 1 hr 10 mins

Servings: 6

Yield: 6 bowls

Ingredients

- 3 tablespoons olive oil
- 8 ounces pancetta bacon, diced
- 2 medium (blank)s red bell peppers, chopped
- 1 onion, chopped
- 4 cloves garlic, minced
- 2 tablespoons coarse kosher salt, or to taste
- 1 tablespoon ground black pepper, or to taste
- 1 tablespoon dried basil
- 1 tablespoon dried thyme
- 1 bay leaf
- 1 (32 ounce) carton low-sodium chicken broth
- 3 ounces tomato paste
- 4 large boneless, skinless chicken breasts
- 2 (14 ounce) cans artichoke hearts, drained and chopped

Directions

Step 1

Heat oil in a large pot over medium-low heat. Add pancetta; cook, stirring occasionally, until golden and crispy, about 10 minutes. Transfer pancetta to a bowl with a slotted spoon; cover and set aside.

Step 2

Stir red bell peppers, onion, garlic, and salt into the same pot. Cook and stir, scraping up the bits from the bottom of the pan, until softened, about 5 minutes. Stir black pepper, basil, thyme, and bay leaf into the pot. Add chicken stock and tomato paste; stir well to combine.

Step 3

Nestle chicken breasts into the pot, submerging them in the stock. Increase heat to medium and bring to a low boil. Reduce heat and simmer stew until chicken is cooked through, stirring occasionally, 15 to 20 minutes. An instant-read thermometer inserted into the center of the chicken should read at least 165 degrees F (74 degrees C).

Step 4

Pull chicken out of the pot and let cool until easily handled, about 10 minutes. Stir artichokes into the stew. Shred or cut up chicken into small pieces and return to pot. Simmer stew until chicken pieces are heated through, about 5 minutes. Ladle into bowls and garnish with pancetta.

Nutrition Facts

Per Serving:

374.3 calories; protein 40.4g 81% DV; carbohydrates 18g 6% DV; fat 15.5g 24% DV; cholesterol 93.9mg 31% DV; sodium 2936.1mg 117% DV.

Peach Pork Picante

Prep: 10 mins **Cook:** 20 mins **Total:** 30 mins

Servings: 6

Yield: 6 servings

Ingredients

- 1 pound boneless pork loin, cubed
- 1 (1 ounce) package taco seasoning mix
- 1 cup salsa
- 4 tablespoons peach preserves

Directions

Step 1

Season pork with taco seasoning. Heat oil in a large skillet over medium high heat. Add seasoned pork and saute until browned, 5 to 7 minutes. Add salsa and peach preserves and mix well. Cover skillet and reduce heat. Let simmer gently for about 10 minutes and serve.

Nutrition Facts

Per Serving:

132.7 calories; protein 9.9g 20% DV; carbohydrates 15.1g 5% DV; fat 3.4g 5% DV; cholesterol 23.4mg 8% DV; sodium 617.5mg 25% DV.

Sweet and Sour Chicken

Prep: 10 mins **Cook:** 20 mins **Total:** 30 mins

Servings: 6

Yield: 6 servings

Ingredients

- 1 (20 ounce) can pineapple chunks, juice reserved
- ¼ cup soy sauce
- ½ cup vinegar
- ¾ cup brown sugar
- ¼ cup all-purpose flour
- 1 ½ medium (blank)s green bell peppers, diced
- 1 cup chopped celery
- 1 (8 ounce) can water chestnuts, drained and sliced
- 1 ½ pounds cooked chicken meat, cut into strips

Directions

Step 1

In a large saucepan over medium-low heat, blend reserved pineapple juice, soy sauce, vinegar, and brown sugar. Mix in flour, and stir until thickened.

Step 2

Stir bell peppers, celery, and water chestnuts into the saucepan. Mix in chicken. Cook and stir until heated through. Stir in the pineapple chunks before serving.

Nutrition Facts

Per Serving:

418 calories; protein 33.3g 67% DV; carbohydrates 53.2g 17% DV; fat 7.9g 12% DV; cholesterol 94.2mg 31% DV; sodium 710.3mg 28% DV.

Authentic Thai Basil Chicken (Very Easy and Fast)

Prep: 15 mins **Cook:** 9 mins **Total:** 24 mins

Servings: 2

Yield: 2 servings

Ingredients

- 2 tablespoons vegetable oil
- ½ onion, sliced
- 3 cloves garlic, sliced
- 1 large skinless, boneless chicken breast, cut into 1-inch pieces
- ¼ cup oyster sauce
- 3 tablespoons soy sauce
- 1 pinch white sugar
- 2 peppers small chile peppers, sliced
- ⅓ cup water
- ½ cup fresh basil leaves

Directions

Step 1

Heat oil in a wok or large skillet over medium heat. Add onion and garlic; cook and stir until fragrant, about 30 seconds. Add chicken; cook and stir until no longer pink, about 5 minutes. Stir in oyster sauce, soy sauce, and sugar. Stir in chile peppers. Pour in water. Cook until slightly thickened, 3 to 5 minutes. Stir in basil before serving.

Cook's Note:

Substitute red pepper flakes for the chile peppers, or omit if you don't like spicy food.

The favorite ingredient in this dish is the fresh basil. Just stir it in and serve. Don't overcook it!

Nutrition Facts

Per Serving:

303.7 calories; protein 25.8g 52% DV; carbohydrates 14.5g 5% DV; fat 16.2g 25% DV; cholesterol 58.5mg 20% DV; sodium 1625.4mg 65% DV.

Bo Kho (Spicy Vietnamese Beef Stew)

Prep: 40 mins **Cook:** 2 hrs 57 mins **Additional:** 30 mins **Total:** 4 hrs 7 mins

Servings: 8

Yield: 8 servings

Ingredients

- 1 stalk lemongrass
- 3 tablespoons fish sauce (patis)
- 2 ½ tablespoons grated ginger
- 2 tablespoons unsweetened applesauce
- 1 ½ teaspoons curry powder
- 1 teaspoon Chinese five-spice powder
- 1 bay leaf
- 2 ½ pounds beef brisket, cut into 1 1/2-inch chunks
- 3 tablespoons ghee (clarified butter)
- 1 onion, finely chopped
- 2 (14.5 ounce) cans diced tomatoes, drained and crushed with your hands
- kosher salt to taste
- 3 cups water
- 1 pound carrots, peeled and chopped into 1-inch pieces
- ¼ cup chopped fresh cilantro

Directions

Step 1

Trim ends off lemongrass and cut into 3-inch pieces. Pound gently with a heavy object until bruised.

Step 2

Mix lemongrass stalk, fish sauce, ginger, applesauce, curry powder, five-spice powder, and bay leaf in a large bowl. Add beef; mix until coated. Let marinate in the refrigerator, about 30 minutes.

Step 3

Preheat oven to 300 degrees F (150 degrees C).

Step 4

Drain excess marinade off beef, reserving lemongrass and bay leaf.

Step 5

Melt ghee in a Dutch oven over medium-high heat. Cook beef in batches until browned, about 30 seconds per side. Transfer beef to a plate. Reduce heat to medium-low. Add onion; cook and stir until soft, about 5 minutes. Stir in tomatoes and salt. Simmer until thickened into a paste, 12 to 14 minutes.

Step 6

Stir beef, reserved lemongrass, and bay leaf into the tomato paste. Increase heat to medium and cook, stirring often, until flavors combine, about 5 minutes. Increase heat to high. Add water and carrots; bring to a boil.

Step 7

Cover and cook in the preheated oven until beef is tender, about 2 1/2 hours. Garnish with cilantro.

Cook's Notes:

Use another cheap cut of beef instead of brisket if desired.

Substitute butter for the ghee if desired.

Substitute 2 whole star anise for the Chinese Five-Spice Powder if preferred. Add them with the lemongrass and bay leaf in **step 4**.

Keep your ginger in the freezer for super-easy grating.

Nutrition Facts

Per Serving:

346.4 calories; protein 16.7g 33% DV; carbohydrates 13.5g 4% DV; fat 24.6g 38% DV; cholesterol 70.6mg 24% DV; sodium 701.9mg 28% DV.

White Chicken Chili with Rice

Prep: 20 mins **Cook:** 20 mins **Total:** 40 mins

Servings: 14

Yield: 14 cups

Ingredients

- 2 pounds roasted chicken, cut into bite-size pieces
- 2 (14 ounce) cans fat-free chicken broth
- 4 cups hot water
- 1 (15 ounce) can navy beans
- 2 (5.6 ounce) packages creamy chicken-flavored rice mix (such as Knorr Rice Side)
- ½ head broccoli, coarsely chopped
- 2 large carrots, sliced 1/4 inch thick
- 1 red bell pepper, cut into 1-inch chunks

Directions

Step 1

Combine chicken, chicken broth, water, navy beans, chicken-flavored rice mix, broccoli, carrots, and red bell pepper in a large Dutch oven. Bring to a boil; reduce heat to low and simmer until broccoli and carrots are tender, about 15 minutes.

Nutrition Facts

Per Serving:

224.8 calories; protein 22.2g 44% DV; carbohydrates 11.3g 4% DV; fat 9.7g 15% DV; cholesterol 55.7mg 19% DV; sodium 319.7mg 13% DV.

Brussels Sprouts 'n Gnocchi

Prep: 15 mins **Cook:** 17 mins **Total:** 32 mins

Servings: 4

Yield: 4 servings

Ingredients

- 1 tablespoon olive oil, or more to taste
- 1 pound fresh Brussels sprouts, thinly sliced
- ¼ small onion, finely chopped
- 1 clove garlic, minced
- 1 pinch salt and ground black pepper to taste
- ¼ cup water, or more as needed
- 1 (16 ounce) package frozen gnocchi
- 1 squeeze lemon juice
- 1 pinch red pepper flakes

Directions

Step 1

Heat olive oil in a large skillet over medium heat. Add Brussels sprouts and onion; cook and stir until onion starts to turn translucent, about 5 minutes. Stir in garlic, salt, and pepper.

Step 2

Pour water and gnocchi into the skillet; cover and simmer until water is absorbed and gnocchi are tender, about 10 minutes. Increase heat to medium-high; cook and stir gnocchi until are browned, 2 to 3 minutes. Stir in lemon juice and red pepper flakes.

Nutrition Facts

Per Serving:

195.9 calories; protein 3g 6% DV; carbohydrates 20.9g 7% DV; fat 11.4g 18% DV; cholesterol 21.3mg 7% DV; sodium 124.9mg 5% DV.

Chili Lime Chicken Tacos

Prep: 15 mins **Cook:** 20 mins **Total:** 35 mins

Servings: 4

Yield: 4 servings

Ingredients

- 1 pound boneless, skinless chicken breasts, cut into bite-size pieces
- 2 tablespoons olive oil, divided
- 1 ½ teaspoons chili powder
- 1 clove garlic, finely chopped
- 2 tablespoons fresh lime juice
- 1 medium poblano pepper, chopped
- 1 small red onion, chopped
- 1 (5.5 ounce) package Knorr Rice Sides - Rice Pilaf
- 8 eaches corn tortillas or taco shells

Directions

Step 1

Season chicken, if desired, with salt and pepper. Combine 1 tablespoon olive oil with chili powder in large bowl; add chicken and toss to coat.

Step 2

Heat large nonstick skillet over medium heat and cook chicken, stirring frequently, until thoroughly cooked, about 6 minutes. Add garlic to skillet and cook, stirring, until fragrant, about 30 seconds. Add lime juice; toss. Remove and set aside.

Step 3

Heat remaining 1 tablespoon oil in same skillet over medium-high heat and cook poblano pepper and onion, stirring occasionally, until softened, about 4 minutes. Add 2 cups water to skillet and Knorr Rice Sides™ - Rice Pilaf and cook according to package **directions**. Stir in chicken.

Step 4

Serve in corn tortillas or taco shells and serve, if desired, with sour cream, lime wedges and salsa verde.

Nutrition Facts

Per Serving:

453 calories; protein 30.3g 61% DV; carbohydrates 56.5g 18% DV; fat 11.8g 18% DV; cholesterol 64.6mg 22% DV; sodium 488.4mg 20% DV.

Mama's Old-Fashioned Albondigas (Meatball Soup)

Prep: 40 mins **Cook:** 45 mins **Total:** 1 hr 25 mins

Servings: 12

Yield: 12 servings

Ingredients

Stock:

- 1 gallon water
- 3 cups tomato sauce
- 1 yellow onion, quartered
- 4 tablespoons chicken bouillon (such as Knorr)
- 3 cloves garlic, minced
- 1 tablespoon dried oregano

Meatballs:

- 3 pounds lean ground beef
- 3 large eggs eggs
- ½ cup tomato sauce
- ¼ cup uncooked white rice
- ¼ cup chopped fresh cilantro
- 1 tablespoon seasoned salt (such as Season-All)
- 1 tablespoon dried oregano leaves
- ½ teaspoon onion powder
- ½ teaspoon garlic powder
- ¼ teaspoon ground black pepper
- ¼ teaspoon ground cumin
- 10 small baby potatoes
- 5 large carrots, sliced diagonally
- 5 stalks celery, sliced diagonally
- 2 eaches zucchini, chopped
- 2 cups thickly shredded green cabbage
- 1 lemon, sliced into wedges
- 2 eaches avocados, chopped
- ¼ cup chopped fresh cilantro

Directions

Step 1

Pour water into a large stockpot over high heat. Stir in 3 cups tomato sauce, yellow onion, chicken bouillon, garlic, and 1 tablespoon dried oregano. Bring broth to a slow boil.

Step 2

Combine ground beef, eggs, 1/2 cup tomato sauce, white rice, 1/4 cup cilantro, seasoned salt, 1 tablespoon dried oregano, onion powder, garlic powder, black pepper, and cumin in a large bowl. Squeeze mixture with your hands until thoroughly mixed.

Step 3

Scoop 1/4 cup of beef mixture and form in a ball. Lower gently into boiling broth. Repeat with remaining beef mixture.

Step 4

Stir potatoes, carrots, and celery into the broth. Cover and simmer until meatballs and potatoes are tender, about 30 minutes. Stir in zucchini and cabbage. Cover and simmer until cabbage is tender, about 10 minutes.

Step 5

Serve with a squeeze of lemon juice and garnish with avocado and 1/4 cup cilantro.

Cook's Notes:

Vegetables can be varied to your liking (corn, bell peppers, squash, etc).

Lean ground beef is preferred for a healthier, less fatty stock. Chicken broth can be substituted for the water and chicken bouillon for a richer stock, if preferred.

Nutrition Facts

Per Serving:

368.6 calories; protein 29.2g 58% DV; carbohydrates 29.5g 10% DV; fat 15.3g 24% DV; cholesterol 127.8mg 43% DV; sodium 1125.3mg 45% DV.

Cilantro Chicken and Rice

Prep: 20 mins **Cook:** 40 mins **Total:** 1 hr

Servings: 8

Yield: 8 servings

Ingredients

- ¼ cup olive oil
- 8 breast half, bone and skin removed (blank)s skinless, boneless chicken breast halves
- ½ cup all-purpose flour
- 1 medium onion, diced
- 1 red bell pepper, diced
- 4 cloves garlic, minced
- 2 cups chicken broth
- 1 (10 ounce) package yellow rice
- 1 (28 ounce) can stewed tomatoes
- 1 (15 ounce) can pinto beans, drained and rinsed
- 1 (15 ounce) can black beans, drained and rinsed
- 1 (15 ounce) can whole kernel corn, drained
- 1 (4 ounce) can diced green chile peppers, drained
- ¾ cup coarsely chopped fresh cilantro
- 1 teaspoon salt
- ½ teaspoon pepper
- ¼ teaspoon ground cayenne pepper

Directions

Step 1

Heat the olive oil in a large skillet over medium heat. Dredge chicken in flour to coat. Place chicken in the skillet, and cook just until browned on all sides; set aside.

Step 2

Stir onion, bell pepper, and garlic into the skillet. Cook 5 minutes, until tender. Pour in chicken broth. Mix in the yellow rice, stewed tomatoes, pinto beans, black beans, corn, diced green chile peppers, and cilantro. Season with salt, pepper, and cayenne pepper. Bring to a boil. Return chicken to skillet. Reduce heat to low, cover, and simmer 30 minutes, until rice is tender and chicken juices run clear.

Nutrition Facts

Per Serving:

439.8 calories; protein 30.8g 62% DV; carbohydrates 57.8g 19% DV; fat 10.5g 16% DV; cholesterol 60.9mg 20% DV; sodium 1539.9mg 62% DV.

Spicy Chicken and Hominy Mexican Soup

Prep: 20 mins **Cook:** 50 mins **Total:** 1 hr 10 mins

Servings: 4

Yield: 4 servings

Ingredients

- 1 tablespoon olive oil
- 2 eaches chicken breasts, cut into 1-inch pieces
- 1 small onion, chopped
- 2 peppers chipotle peppers in adobo sauce, seeded and diced
- 2 cloves garlic, minced
- 1 pinch garlic salt, or to taste
- 1 (32 ounce) can enchilada sauce
- 2 (16 ounce) cans hominy
- 1 (15 ounce) can diced tomatoes
- 1 (15 ounce) can black beans, rinsed and drained
- 1 ½ cups water
- 2 tablespoons chili powder
- 1 tablespoon ground cumin
- 1 teaspoon dried oregano
- 1 pinch cayenne pepper
- salt and ground black pepper to taste
- ¼ cup chopped cilantro

Directions

Step 1

Heat oil in a large pot over medium-high heat. Add chicken, onion, chipotle peppers, garlic, and garlic salt; cook and stir until lightly browned, 5 to 8 minutes.

Step 2

Stir enchilada sauce, hominy, tomatoes, black beans, and water into the pot. Season with chili powder, cumin, oregano, cayenne pepper, salt, and pepper. Bring to a gentle boil. Cover and simmer until flavors combine, about 40 minutes. Garnish with cilantro.

Nutrition Facts

Per Serving:

693.2 calories; protein 25.2g 50% DV; carbohydrates 68.2g 22% DV; fat 36.4g 56% DV; cholesterol 112mg 37% DV; sodium 1308.6mg 52% DV.

Crema di Cavolo Romanesco (Romanesco Broccoli Soup)

Prep: 25 mins **Cook:** 42 mins **Total:** 1 hr 7 mins

Servings: 2

Yield: 2 servings

Ingredients

- 2 tablespoons extra-virgin olive oil
- 1 small carrot, finely chopped
- 1 shallot, finely chopped
- ½ rib celery, finely chopped
- 3 ½ ounces Romanesco broccoli, tough parts discarded, chopped
- 2 small potatoes, peeled and chopped
- 4 cups hot water
- salt and ground black pepper to taste

Directions

Step 1

Heat olive oil in a saucepan over medium-low heat. Add carrot, shallot, and celery; cook and stir until fragrant, 2 to 3 minutes. Add Romanesco broccoli and potatoes.

Step 2

Pour hot water into the saucepan. Season with salt and pepper. Cook, covered, until broccoli and potatoes are soft, about 40 minutes. Puree soup with an immersion blender until smooth.

Cook's Notes:

You can serve as-is or add some grilled prawns on top.

Puree soup in a food processor instead of using an immersion blender if preferred.

Nutrition Facts

Per Serving:

295.5 calories; protein 5.4g 11% DV; carbohydrates 39.4g 13% DV; fat 13.8g 21% DV; cholesterolmg; sodium 149.7mg 6% DV.

Spicy Cayenne Tomato Jam

Prep: 20 mins **Cook:** 3 hrs **Additional:** 1 hr **Total:** 4 hrs 20 mins

Servings: 32

Yield: 4 cups

Ingredients

- 4 pounds tomatoes, peeled and chopped
- 1 large apple, peeled and chopped
- 1 cup raw sugar
- 1 yellow onion, diced
- ½ cup brown sugar
- ¼ cup apple cider vinegar
- 3 tablespoons lemon juice
- 1 teaspoon salt
- ½ teaspoon ground cayenne pepper, or more to taste

Directions

Step 1

Combine tomatoes, apple, sugar, onion, brown sugar, apple cider vinegar, lemon juice, salt, and cayenne in a large pot; bring to a boil. Reduce heat and simmer, stirring occasionally, until dark and syrupy, about 2 hours 30 minutes. Continue simmering until mixture thickens to a jam-like consistency, about 30 minutes more.

Step 2

Remove jam from heat and cool to room temperature, 1 to 2 hours. Transfer to lidded containers and refrigerate.

Cook's Note:

Add more cayenne if necessary to reach desired spice level.

Jam will keep for several weeks in the refrigerator or you can process for long-term storage.

Nutrition Facts

Per Serving:

51.8 calories; protein 0.6g 1% DV; carbohydrates 12.9g 4% DV; fat 0.1g; cholesterolmg; sodium 79.2mg 3% DV.

Zucchini Fenchel Suppe (Zucchini and Fennel Soup)

Prep: 20 mins **Cook:** 18 mins **Total:** 38 mins

Servings: 4

Yield: 4 servings

Ingredients

- 2 tablespoons butter
- 1 onion, finely chopped
- 1 bulb fennel, diced, green tops reserved
- 1 zucchini, peeled and thinly sliced
- 2 cups chicken stock
- 1 teaspoon mild curry powder
- salt and freshly ground black pepper to taste
- 1 teaspoon white wine vinegar, or to taste

Directions

Step 1

Melt butter in a large pot over medium heat. Add onion; cook and stir until softened, about 5 minutes. Add fennel bulb and zucchini; cook, stirring occasionally, for 3 minutes. Pour in chicken stock. Reduce heat to low and simmer soup, covered, until fennel is soft, 10 to 15 minutes.

Step 2

Puree soup with an immersion blender until smooth. Season with curry powder, salt, and black pepper. Add white wine vinegar.

Step 3

Chop reserved fennel tops finely and sprinkle over soup before serving.

Cook's Note:

If soup appears too thick in **step 2**, thin with a little water or more stock.

Nutrition Facts

Per Serving:

103.4 calories; protein 2.1g 4% DV; carbohydrates 11.4g 4% DV; fat 6.4g 10% DV; cholesterol 15.6mg 5% DV; sodium 458.5mg 18% DV.

Kickin' Vegetarian Collard Greens

Prep: 20 mins **Cook:** 40 mins **Total:** 1 hr

Servings: 6

Yield: 6 servings

Ingredients

- 1 tablespoon olive oil
- 1 tablespoon butter
- 1 large onion, halved and thinly sliced
- 4 cloves garlic, thinly sliced
- 2 sprigs fresh thyme, leaves stripped
- 2 eaches bay leaves
- 2 (14 ounce) cans chopped tomatoes
- 1 cup vegetable broth
- 1 tablespoon brown sugar
- 1 tablespoon molasses
- 1 tablespoon liquid smoke flavoring
- 2 pounds collard greens, chopped
- 1 ½ cups cooked white beans

Directions

Step 1

Heat olive oil and butter in a large pot over medium heat until butter melts and starts to brown, 1 to 2 minutes. Add onion and garlic; cook and stir until onion turns translucent, about 5 minutes. Stir in thyme and bay leaves.

Step 2

Pour chopped tomatoes, vegetable broth, brown sugar, molasses, and liquid smoke into the pot; bring to a simmer. Stir in collard greens gently. Reduce heat to low and simmer, covered, until tender, about 30 minutes.

Cook's Notes:

If you're not planning to serve the collard greens with black-eyed peas, the white beans (or chickpeas) can be added at the same time as the tomatoes to make this a main dish, served of course with corn bread on the side.

Substitute 1/2 teaspoon dried thyme for the fresh thyme if desired.

Nutrition Facts

Per Serving:

237.8 calories; protein 10.3g 21% DV; carbohydrates 35.1g 11% DV; fat 7.5g 12% DV; cholesterol 5.1mg 2% DV; sodium 335.1mg 13% DV.

Caribbean Dream Chili

Prep: 10 mins **Cook:** 1 hr 15 mins **Total:** 1 hr 25 mins

Servings: 8

Yield: 8 servings

Ingredients

- 2 tablespoons vegetable oil
- 1 small onion, chopped
- 2 tablespoons bottled minced garlic
- 1 pound ground pork
- 1 pound ground sirloin
- 1 (28 ounce) can whole peeled tomatoes
- 2 cups low-sodium beef broth
- 1 (15 ounce) can black beans, rinsed and drained
- ½ cup golden raisins
- 2 tablespoons chili powder
- 1 teaspoon ground cumin
- 1 teaspoon ground cinnamon
- 1 teaspoon salt
- ½ teaspoon ground allspice
- ¼ teaspoon ground cloves
- ¼ cup halved green olives
- ¼ cup slivered almonds

Directions

Step 1

Heat oil in a large pot over medium heat. Cook and stir onion and garlic until soft, about 2 minutes. Stir in pork and sirloin; cook and stir until browned, 8 to 10 minutes. Drain excess grease from the pot.

Step 2

Crush tomatoes by hand and add them to the pot with their juices. Pour in beef broth. Stir in black beans, raisins, chili powder, cumin, cinnamon, salt, allspice, and cloves. Bring to a boil; reduce heat and simmer, covered, until raisins are soft, about 30 minutes.

Step 3

Stir green olives and almonds into the pot. Simmer until flavors combine, about 30 minutes.

Nutrition Facts

Per Serving:

391.8 calories; protein 26.3g 53% DV; carbohydrates 24.1g 8% DV; fat 21.7g 33% DV; cholesterol 71.2mg 24% DV; sodium 864.8mg 35% DV.

Artichoke and Chicken Sausage Cauliflower "Paella"

Prep: 25 mins **Cook:** 27 mins **Additional:** 3 mins **Total:** 55 mins

Servings: 4

Yield: 4 servings

Ingredients

- 1 head cauliflower, broken into florets
- 2 tablespoons hot water
- ½ teaspoon saffron threads
- ¼ cup extra-virgin olive oil , divided
- 3 links sweet Italian chicken sausage, diced
- 1 large zucchini, chopped
- 1 yellow onion, chopped
- 1 carrot, grated
- 2 cloves garlic, or more to taste, minced
- ¼ teaspoon ground cayenne pepper
- 1 (15 ounce) can artichokes, drained
- 3 cups chicken stock
- sea salt
- ½ teaspoon freshly ground black pepper
- 1 ½ cups snow peas

Directions

Step 1

Place cauliflower florets in a food processor; pulse into grains the size of rice.

Step 2

Combine hot water and saffron threads in a small bowl; let stand for 3 minutes to infuse.

Step 3

Heat 2 tablespoons olive oil in a paella pan over medium heat. Add sausage; cook and stir until browned, about 5 minutes. Stir in zucchini and onion; cook for 3 minutes. Add saffron infusion, carrot, garlic, and cayenne pepper; cook for 1 minute.

Step 4

Stir cauliflower "rice" and artichokes into the pan. Cook and stir until slightly softened, about 3 minutes. Pour in stock; season with salt and pepper. Bring to a boil; reduce heat and simmer until most of the stock is absorbed, about 10 minutes. Stir in snow peas; simmer until all stock is absorbed, 3 to 5 minutes more.

Step 5

Remove paella from the heat and drizzle remaining 2 tablespoons olive oil on top.

Cook's Notes:

Substitute vegetable stock for the chicken stock if desired.

Use mild or hot sausage as preferred.

Nutrition Facts

Per Serving:

427.3 calories; protein 18.1g 36% DV; carbohydrates 32g 10% DV; fat 26.9g 42% DV; cholesterol 25.6mg 9% DV; sodium 2195.6mg 88% DV.

Portuguese Shrimp

Prep: 20 mins **Cook:** 25 mins **Total:** 45 mins

Servings: 8

Yield: 8 servings

Ingredients

- 1 tablespoon extra-virgin olive oil, or more as needed
- 1 onion, chopped
- 3 cloves garlic, minced
- 1 (12 fluid ounce) can ale, divided
- 5 sprigs parsley, stemmed and chopped
- 2 teaspoons tomato paste
- 2 teaspoons Portuguese hot pepper sauce (pimenta)
- 1 cube chicken bouillon
- 1 teaspoon ground paprika
- 2 pounds unpeeled large shrimp, deveined
- 1 teaspoon kosher salt

Directions

Step 1

Heat olive oil in a large skillet over medium heat. Add onion and garlic; cook and stir until softened, about 5 minutes. Stir in parsley, tomato paste, hot pepper sauce, chicken bouillon, and paprika. Pour in half of the ale; simmer until flavors combine, about 5 minutes.

Step 2

Pour remaining ale into the skillet; add shrimp. Season with salt. Cook until shrimp absorbs the liquid and turns pink, 15 to 20 minutes.

Nutrition Facts

Per Serving:

147.2 calories; protein 19.9g 40% DV; carbohydrates 6.3g 2% DV; fat 2.9g 4% DV; cholesterol 172.9mg 58% DV; sodium 614mg 25% DV.

Portuguese Sopas

Prep: 15 mins **Cook:** 4 hrs 30 mins **Total:** 4 hrs 45 mins

Servings: 8

Yield: 8 servings

Ingredients

- 1 (3 pound) beef pot roast
- 1 onion, diced
- 1 cup fresh mint leaves
- 2 cloves garlic, minced, or more to taste
- 2 teaspoons ground cinnamon
- 2 teaspoons ground allspice
- 2 eaches bay leaves, or more to taste
- salt and ground black pepper to taste
- water to cover

- 1 head cabbage, quartered, or more to taste

Directions

Step 1

Place pot roast, onion, mint, garlic, cinnamon, allspice, and bay leaves in a large pot. Season with salt and pepper. Pour in enough water to cover the roast. Cook over medium heat until roast is tender, adding more water if needed, about 4 hours.

Step 2

Stir cabbage wedges into the pot. Simmer until cabbage is tender, about 30 minutes.

Cook's Note:

As a variation, I will add various root vegetables. My favorites are red and white beets, and/or carrots.

You can also make this in a slow cooker; cook on Low, 6 to 7 hours. Add cabbage in the last 1/2 hour.

Nutrition Facts

Per Serving:

464.4 calories; protein 33.8g 68% DV; carbohydrates 11.1g 4% DV; fat 31.5g 49% DV; cholesterol 115.8mg 39% DV; sodium 149.3mg 6% DV.

Osso Bucco-Style Beef Shank

Prep: 10 mins **Cook:** 1 hr 50 mins **Total:** 2 hrs

Servings: 2

Yield: 2 servings

Ingredients

- 2 tablespoons olive oil
- 1 onion, chopped
- 3 cloves garlic, chopped
- 1 pound beef shank
- ¼ teaspoon dried thyme
- ¼ teaspoon dried oregano
- ¼ teaspoon dried rosemary
- ¼ teaspoon dried marjoram
- 1 (16 ounce) can diced tomatoes
- 1 (6 ounce) can tomato paste

- water
- 1 tablespoon lemon zest
- 1 teaspoon sea salt
- ½ teaspoon coarsely ground black pepper

Directions

Step 1

Heat olive oil in a large saucepan over medium heat. Add onion and garlic; cook and stir until softened, about 5 minutes. Transfer to a plate. Increase heat to medium-high. Add beef shank and cook until browned, about 5 minutes per side. Return onion and garlic to the pan. Sprinkle thyme, oregano, rosemary, and marjoram over beef.

Step 2

Pour tomatoes and tomato paste into the pan. Fill the empty tomato paste can with water and pour into the pan. Stir in lemon zest, salt, and black pepper. Bring to a boil; reduce heat to low and simmer, covered, until beef is very tender, 1 1/2 to 2 hours.

Cook's Notes:

Substitute 4 fresh tomatoes - blanched, peeled and diced - for the canned tomatoes if desired.

Towards the end, you can add your favorite vegetable to the pot (I like spinach with this, although it does get soggy).

Nutrition Facts

Per Serving:

519.9 calories; protein 36.8g 74% DV; carbohydrates 32.7g 11% DV; fat 28.9g 44% DV; cholesterol 79.2mg 26% DV; sodium 1931.1mg 77% DV.

Grandmum's Fish Ball Soup

Prep: 40 mins **Cook:** 40 mins **Total:** 1 hr 20 mins

Servings: 6

Yield: 6 servings

Ingredients

- 1 tablespoon vegetable oil, or to taste
- 2 eaches red onions, chopped
- 5 cloves garlic, sliced
- ½ inch piece fresh ginger root, sliced

- ½ teaspoon Chinese pickled cabbage (tung choy)
- 9 ounces boneless chicken breast, cubed
- 11 ounces medium shrimp, cleaned and deveined
- 30 eaches fish balls
- 4 ounces lotus root, thinly sliced
- ground white pepper to taste
- 6 cups chicken stock
- 5 ounces baby choy sum, leaves and stalks separated
- 5 ounces baby bok choy, leaves and stalks separated
- 2 peppers red chile peppers, sliced
- salt to taste

Directions

Step 1

Heat oil in a large pot or wok over medium heat. Add onions, garlic, and ginger; cook and stir until translucent, about 5 minutes. Stir in pickled cabbage. Add chicken; cook and stir until juices run clear, about 5 minutes. Add shrimp; cook and stir until starting to turn pink, about 2 minutes. Add fish balls and lotus root. Season with white pepper.

Step 2

Pour chicken stock into the pot. Bring to a boil; reduce heat and simmer until fish balls float and lotus root is slightly tender, about 10 minutes. Stir in choy sum and bok choy stalks. Continue simmering until slightly softened, about 5 minutes.

Step 3

Stir choy sum and bok choy leaves, chile peppers, salt into the pot. Simmer until leaves are wilted and flavors combine, about 5 minutes.

Cook's Note:

You can omit the preserved vegetables if you can't find them.

Nutrition Facts

Per Serving:

784.2 calories; protein 62.5g 125% DV; carbohydrates 50.5g 16% DV; fat 37.5g 58% DV; cholesterol 275.7mg 92% DV; sodium 1729mg 69% DV.

Chinese Stir-Fried Sticky Rice with Chinese Sausage

Prep: 15 mins **Cook:** 36 mins **Additional:** 4 hrs 15 mins **Total:** 5 hrs 6 mins

Servings: 6

Yield: 6 servings

Ingredients

- 2 cups glutinous rice
- 8 eaches dried shiitake mushrooms
- ⅓ cup dried shrimp
- 2 eaches dried scallops
- 1 teaspoon olive oil
- 3 large eggs eggs, beaten
- 3 links Chinese sausage, diced
- 2 cups hot water, or more as needed
- 2 tablespoons light soy sauce, or to taste
- 2 teaspoons dark soy sauce
- 1 teaspoon white sugar
- ½ cup chopped cilantro, or to taste

Directions

Step 1

Soak rice in a large bowl of water until mostly translucent, about 4 hours. Rinse and drain thoroughly.

Step 2

Soak mushrooms, shrimp, and scallops in 3 separate bowls of water until softened, about 15 minutes. Drain, reserving mushroom water and discarding other water. Chop mushrooms, shrimp, and scallops into small pieces.

Step 3

Heat olive oil in a large skillet over medium heat. Pour eggs into skillet, swirling to spread out into a thin layer. Cook until mostly firm, about 1 minute. Flip and cook until no longer runny, 3 to 5 minutes.

Step 4

Transfer egg to a cutting board and allow to cool slightly. Roll into a long tube and slice into thin ribbons.

Step 5

Stir Chinese sausage into the same skillet over medium heat. Cook and stir until fragrant and some of the oil is released, about 3 minutes. Add mushrooms, shrimp, and scallops; cook for 3 to 5 minutes. Transfer sausage mixture to a bowl.

Step 6

Stir drained rice into the skillet. Cook and stir until lightly toasted, 1 to 2 minutes. Pour in reserved mushroom water, stirring constantly until water is absorbed. Add hot water, 1/2 cup at a time, stirring until water is absorbed between each addition. Cook until rice is softened, about 25 minutes.

Step 7

Season rice with light soy sauce, dark soy sauce, and sugar. Stir in egg ribbons and sausage mixture. Top with cilantro before serving.

Nutrition Facts

Per Serving:

544.5 calories; protein 21.8g 44% DV; carbohydrates 82.8g 27% DV; fat 16.4g 25% DV; cholesterol 103.5mg 35% DV; sodium 830.6mg 33% DV.

Bacon Cider Chili

Prep: 10 mins **Cook:** 1 hr 2 mins **Total:** 1 hr 12 mins

Servings: 8

Yield: 8 servings

Ingredients

- 3 slices thick-cut bacon, chopped
- 1 large onion, chopped
- 4 garlic clove (blank)s garlic cloves, minced
- 2 pounds lean ground beef
- 1 tablespoon chili powder
- 1 teaspoon smoked Spanish paprika
- 1 teaspoon salt
- ¼ teaspoon cayenne pepper
- 1 (14.5 ounce) can fire-roasted diced tomatoes
- 1 ½ cups hard apple cider (such as Samuel Smith)
- 1 (8 ounce) can tomato sauce
- 1 teaspoon Worcestershire sauce
- 1 (14.5 ounce) can pinto beans, drained

Directions

Step 1

Place bacon in a large pot over medium-high heat; cook until starting to brown, about 5 minutes. Add onion; reduce heat to medium and cook, covered, stirring occasionally, until translucent, about 5 minutes. Stir in garlic; cook until fragrant, about 1 minute.

Step 2

Increase heat to medium-high and add ground beef to the pot; cook and stir until no longer pink, about 5 minutes. Stir in chili powder, smoked paprika, salt, and cayenne pepper; cook for 1 minute.

Step 3

Pour diced tomatoes, apple cider, tomato sauce, and Worcestershire sauce into the pot. Bring to a boil; reduce heat to medium-low and simmer, covered, until flavors combine, about 30 minutes.

Step 4

Stir pinto beans into the pot. Simmer, uncovered, until beans are heated through, about 10 minutes.

Cook's Note:

Smoked Spanish paprika and fire-roasted crushed tomatoes can be found in most good specialty or gourmet food stores.

Nutrition Facts

Per Serving:

343.1 calories; protein 27.1g 54% DV; carbohydrates 18.3g 6% DV; fat 15.9g 25% DV; cholesterol 82.7mg 28% DV; sodium 896mg 36% DV.

Jessica's Vegetarian Chili

Prep: 35 mins **Cook:** 37 mins **Total:** 1 hr 12 mins

Servings: 6

Yield: 6 servings

Ingredients

- 2 tablespoons olive oil
- 1 yellow onion, chopped
- 3 cloves garlic, minced
- 4 eaches sweet peppers, chopped
- 1 yellow squash, cut into large chunks
- 1 green bell pepper, chopped
- 1 red bell pepper, chopped
- 1 zucchini, cut into large chunks
- 1 tablespoon chili powder
- 1 tablespoon oregano
- 1 tablespoon parsley
- 1 ½ teaspoons ground paprika
- 1 ½ teaspoons ground cumin
- 2 eaches bay leaves
- salt and ground black pepper to taste
- 1 (28 ounce) can crushed tomatoes
- 1 (15 ounce) can kidney beans, rinsed and drained
- 1 (15 ounce) can chili beans
- 1 (14.5 ounce) can diced tomatoes

Directions

Step 1

Heat oil in a large pot over medium-high heat. Saute onion and garlic in the hot oil until onion starts to soften, 2 to 3 minutes. Add sweet peppers, yellow squash, green bell pepper, red bell pepper, zucchini, chili powder, oregano, parsley, paprika, cumin, bay leaves, salt, and pepper; cook and stir for 5 minutes.

Step 2

Stir crushed tomatoes, kidney beans, chili beans, and diced tomatoes into the pot. Reduce heat to medium-low; cook chili, stirring occasionally, until flavors combine, 30 to 45 minutes.

Cook's Note:

You can add meat to this for a heartier chili. I recommend lean ground beef or smoked sausage.

Nutrition Facts

Per Serving:

263 calories; protein 12.2g 25% DV; carbohydrates 45.2g 15% DV; fat 6.4g 10% DV; cholesterol 0.3mg; sodium 796mg 32% DV.

Cheesy Sausage Lasagna Soup

Prep: 20 mins **Cook:** 20 mins **Additional:** 2 mins **Total:** 42 mins

Servings: 6

Yield: 6 servings

Ingredients

- 1 pound Italian turkey sausage, casings removed
- 2 cups chopped onions
- 2 cups sliced fresh mushrooms
- 4 cloves garlic, minced
- 4 cups chicken broth
- 1 (15 ounce) can tomato sauce
- 1 (14.5 ounce) can Italian-seasoned diced tomatoes
- 1 cup uncooked mafalda pasta
- 2 cups chopped fresh spinach
- 1 cup shredded mozzarella cheese
- ¼ cup Parmesan cheese
- 4 teaspoons thinly sliced fresh basil

Directions

Step 1

Cook and stir sausage in a large pot until browned, about 5 minutes. Stir in onions, mushrooms, and garlic. Pour in chicken broth, tomato sauce, and diced tomatoes; bring soup to a boil.

Step 2

Stir pasta into the soup. Cook, stirring occasionally, until almost tender, about 10 minutes. Stir in spinach, mozzarella cheese, and Parmesan cheese. Remove from heat; stir in basil and let stand until pasta is tender, about 2 minutes more.

Cook's Note:

Use any shape pasta you like.

Nutrition Facts

Per Serving:

280.8 calories; protein 24.6g 49% DV; carbohydrates 19.8g 6% DV; fat 12.3g 19% DV; cholesterol 75.4mg 25% DV; sodium 2113.4mg 85% DV.

Chicken Pasta with Artichoke Hearts

Prep: 15 mins **Cook:** 33 mins **Total:** 48 mins

Servings: 4

Yield: 4 servings

Ingredients

- 2 cups penne pasta
- 1 (6 ounce) jar marinated artichokes, coarsely chopped, marinade reserved
- 3 eaches skinless, boneless chicken breasts, cut into bite-sized pieces
- 3 cups sliced fresh mushrooms
- ¾ cup reduced-fat low-sodium chicken broth
- ½ cup dry white wine
- 1 tablespoon cornstarch
- salt and ground black pepper to taste

Directions

Step 1

Bring a large pot of lightly salted water to a boil; add penne and cook, stirring occasionally, until tender yet firm to the bite, about 11 minutes. Drain.

Step 2

Pour artichoke marinade into a large nonstick skillet over medium heat. Add chicken; cook and stir until white, about 3 minutes. Add mushrooms; cook and stir until chicken is no longer pink in the center, 4 to 6 minutes. Stir in artichokes.

Step 3

Mix chicken broth, white wine, and cornstarch together in a bowl until cornstarch is dissolved. Pour into the skillet slowly, stirring constantly until sauce comes to a boil. Reduce heat and simmer until thickened, about 5 minutes.

Step 4

Toss chicken mixture with penne in a large bowl. Season with salt and pepper.

Nutrition Facts

Per Serving:

300.7 calories; protein 24.7g 49% DV; carbohydrates 35.3g 11% DV; fat 5.1g 8% DV; cholesterol 45mg 15% DV; sodium 452mg 18% DV.

Pan-Roasted Red Potatoes

Prep: 5 mins **Cook:** 6 mins **Total:** 11 mins

Servings: 2

Yield: 2 servings

Ingredients

- 1 tablespoon duck fat
- 3 eaches unpeeled red potatoes, diced
- 1 teaspoon dried parsley
- ½ teaspoon salt
- ¼ teaspoon ground white pepper

Directions

Step 1

Melt duck fat in a large skillet over medium-high heat until shimmering, about 1 minute. Add potatoes; cook, stirring minimally, until potatoes are golden brown, 5 to 10 minutes. Drain excess fat.

Step 2

Combine parsley, salt, and white pepper in a bowl; toss over cooked potatoes to coat evenly.

Cook's Notes:

If you are a fan of white pepper, you can increase the amount to 1/2 teaspoon, which is the amount we use when we cook this dish. I dropped it down for the sake of this recipe since not everyone is as big of a fan as we are of the ingredient.

Feel free to use bacon fat instead of duck fat; you can also substitute olive oil for duck fat to make this dish vegetarian.

Nutrition Facts

Per Serving:

97.7 calories; protein 1.2g 2% DV; carbohydrates 9.3g 3% DV; fat 6.5g 10% DV; cholesterol 6.4mg 2% DV; sodium 585.8mg 23% DV.

Easy Lime Cilantro Rice

Prep: 10 mins **Cook:** 25 mins **Total:** 35 mins

Servings: 4

Yield: 4 servings

Ingredients

- ½ cup chopped fresh cilantro
- 2 tablespoons lime juice
- 1 tablespoon olive oil
- 1 teaspoon onion powder
- 1 teaspoon dried parsley
- 1 teaspoon garlic powder
- ½ teaspoon ground cumin
- ¼ teaspoon chili powder
- 2 cups water
- 1 cup basmati rice
- ½ teaspoon salt
- ½ (11 ounce) can Mexican-style corn (such as Green Giant Mexicorn)

Directions

Step 1

Combine cilantro, lime juice, olive oil, onion powder, parsley, garlic powder, ground cumin, and chili powder in a bowl.

Step 2

Bring water to a boil over high heat. Stir in rice and salt. Reduce heat and cover; simmer for 15 minutes, stirring occasionally. Stir in cilantro mixture and Mexican-style corn; simmer over low heat, covered, until corn is heated through, about 5 minutes.

Cook's Notes:

You may process the cilantro lime mixture in a blender; this will make your rice green.

Stir in half of a drained can of Green Giant(R) Mexicorn(R) for added flavor.

Nutrition Facts

Per Serving:

233.9 calories; protein 4.9g 10% DV; carbohydrates 45.7g 15% DV; fat 4.1g 6% DV; cholesterolmg; sodium 512.4mg 21% DV.

Skillet Chicken Picante

Servings: 6

Yield: 6 servings

Ingredients

- 3 breast half, bone and skin removed (blank)s skinless, boneless chicken breasts
- 1 onion, chopped
- 1 tablespoon garlic powder
- 1 tablespoon vegetable oil
- 1 (14.5 ounce) can diced tomatoes
- 1 (24 ounce) jar picante sauce
- 10 (10 inch) flour tortillas
- 12 ounces shredded Cheddar cheese

Directions

Step 1

Cube chicken breasts. Heat oil in a medium skillet. Add cubed chicken breasts, onion and garlic powder and saute until chicken is cooked through and no longer pink, about 15 to 20 minutes. Pour tomatoes and picante sauce over chicken mixture. Let simmer over medium heat until sauce has thickened, usually about 30 minutes. Place some of the mixture in a warm tortilla, add cheese and wrap. Repeat until all of the chicken mixture is gone!

Nutrition Facts

Per Serving:

763.5 calories; protein 40.4g 81% DV; carbohydrates 79g 26% DV; fat 22.1g 34% DV; cholesterol 93.8mg 31% DV; sodium 1897.5mg 76% DV.

Printed in Great Britain
by Amazon